Twenty-Four Short Sermons On The Doctrine Of Universal Salvation

John Bovee Dods

Alpha Editions

This edition published in 2024

ISBN : 9789362517043

Design and Setting By
Alpha Editions
www.alphaedis.com
Email - info@alphaedis.com

As per information held with us this book is in Public Domain.
This book is a reproduction of an important historical work. Alpha Editions uses the best technology to reproduce historical work in the same manner it was first published to preserve its original nature. Any marks or number seen are left intentionally to preserve its true form.

SERMON I

"What man is he that desireth life, and loveth many days that he may see good? Keep thy tongue from evil, and thy lips from speaking guile; depart from evil and do good; seek peace and pursue it." Psalm xxxiv:12-14.

Self-preservation and the desire of protracting the momentary span of life is the first principle of our nature, or is at least so intimately interwoven with our constitution as to appear inherent. So powerful is this desire, that in defiance of pain and misery, it seldom quits us to the last moments of our existence. To endeavor to lengthen out our lives is not only desirable, but is a duty enjoined upon us in the scriptures, and is most beautifully and forcibly expressed in our text.

We might here introduce many observations of a philosophical character on *air* and *climate, meat* and *drink, motion* and *rest, sleeping* and *watching, &c.* and show how sensibly they contribute to health; and we might furnish many examples of long life, but we pass these, and proceed to notice the affections of the mind upon which our text is grounded.

The due regulation of the passions contributes more to health and longevity than climate, or even the observance of any course of diet. Our Creator has so constituted our natures, that *duty, health, happiness* and *longevity* are inseparably blended in the same cup. To suppress, and finally subdue all the passions of malice, anger, envy, jealousy, hatred and revenge, and to exercise (till they become familiar) all the noble passions of tenderness, compassion, love, hope and joy, is a duty that heaven solemnly enjoins upon us, and in the performance of which our years will be multiplied. But we must guard not only our moral natures from the ravages of the corroding and revengeful passions, but also our physical natures by observing the strictest rules of temperance in *eating, drinking, cleanliness* and *exercise.*

The book of God commands us to "be temperate in all things." The observance of this duty gives us a firm constitution, robust health, and prepares us to participate in all the innocent and rational enjoyments of life. Here we may witness the goodness of the Divine Being in uniting our duty, happiness and interest in one; and so firmly are they wedded together, and so absolutely does each depend upon the other that they cannot exist alone. They are alike laid in ruins the moment they are separated. If we trace this idea still further, we witness the same wise arrangement, and the same incomprehensible skill and goodness of the Author of our being in the constitution of our mental natures. In these also he has wholly united our duty, happiness and longevity in one. Jesus says, "Love your enemies; bless them that curse you, do good to them that hate you, and pray for them that despitefully use you, and persecute you, that ye may be the children of your Father in heaven." Paul says—"Let all bitterness and wrath and anger and clamor and evil speaking be put away from you, with all malice, and be ye kind one to another, tender hearted, forgiving one another even as God for Christ's sake hath forgiven you."

Here then is our duty plainly pointed out. If we will exercise this spirit of benignity to our enemies, subdue all our revengeful passions, and indulge a spirit of love and friendship, of meekness and cheerfulness towards our friends and neighbors, we shall not only be happy as our natures can bear, not only revel in all the rational enjoyments this life can impart, but we shall in the common course of providence live to old age. All those, with very few exceptions, who have lived to 80, 90, and 100 years, have been remarked for their equanimity. They were mild spirited, kind, cheerful, and of such a temperament, that neither misfortune, nor any outward circumstances, that agitated the world, could disturb their heaven-born repose.

Thus we see that the path of duty, enjoined in the sacred scriptures, is not only the path of peace and joy, but conducts to a good old age. The goodness of the Divine Being is most strikingly exemplified in uniting health and temperance, happiness and longevity, and our duty to our fellow creatures, all in one.

Long life and good days, however, depend more upon the state of our minds than upon almost any other circumstance. He who lives in fear and trouble arising from any cause whatever; whether from contemplation of endless misery in the future world, or from the apprehension that his earthly prospects will be blasted and his fortune laid in ruins—or if he is continually involved in quarrels, broils and tumults with his neighbors, has but little prospect of living to old age, and certainly no hope of seeing good days. He is in a constant hell. Here then we see the beauty and propriety of our text: "What man is he that desireth life and loveth many days that he may see good? Keep thy tongue from evil and thy lips from speaking guile; depart from evil and do good; seek peace and pursue it."

The first *condition* for a long life is, "keep thy tongue from evil and thy lips from speaking guile." But the question arises, in what sense can the violation of that *condition* have any effect upon the length of life? The answer is at hand—the slanderer is ever a busy body in other men's matters. He is secretly endeavoring to injure his neighbors. He circulates falsehoods about them from house to house. One and another hears the reports put into circulation. They call upon the author for an explanation of his conduct. Involved in trouble, arising from fear, guilt and mortification, he tells a thousand falsehoods to clear up one. All this preys upon his inmost vitals, while perhaps with another, whom he has slandered, he is involved in a quarrel, and it terminates in a settled hatred; and a third case becomes an incurable distemper of rancour and revenge. Here is a man who by slander has rendered his existence wretched. He is like the troubled ocean whose waters find no rest.

There is but little hope of his reaching the common age of man. Instead of seeing good days he is walking in the regions of night and wo. Says the wise man, "where there is no fuel the fire goeth out, so where there is no tattler, strife ceaseth." Yes, "where there is envying and strife, there is confusion and every evil work."

Violent anger excites powerfully the caloric in the human system, boils the blood, and in this state throws it suddenly upon the brain. The powerful shock propels it instantly to the exterior surface, and torrent-like contracts it back again in redoubled fury upon the brain, and leaves the countenance pale and ghastly. It deranges in a great measure the mind, and unfits it for useful action. It darts its electric fire of vengeance along the optic nerve, expands the retina, and gives to every object a magnified and false appearance, while the very eye-balls by a wild and savage glare proclaim the dreadful storm that is raging within, and pouring the poisonous streams of premature death through all the healthful channels of existence! It suddenly braces the nervous system, and then on the opposite extreme leaves it depressed and weakened. It gradually brings on rheumatic complaints, and lays the whole system open to the most formidable and painful disorders that afflict the human race. It cannot have escaped medical observation that fevers and consumptions are much more frequent among persons who are very irritable and exercise little or no rule over their passions, than among those who are of a mild temperament, either naturally, or from early restraint and education.

There is a connexion between the mind and the body so subtle that it has hitherto eluded the eagle-eye of Physiology, and will perhaps remain inscrutable forever to human comprehension. But that this connexion exists is fully demonstrated by medical experience, and observation. Many bodily disorders derange the mind, and have in many instances totally destroyed it. So on the other hand diseases of the mind effect the body in return, and *grief, despair* and *melancholy* have so preyed upon the vitals as to emaciate the body, and bring it to the grave. It is not uncommon that consumptions are brought on by *trouble* of mind, by *guilt*, and by *melancholy* and *grief*. And many instances have occurred, where persons in excessive violent anger have dropped down dead. What is so dreadful, when carried to extreme, must be very injurious to health, and long life, when indulged frequently and even moderately.

There being then such an intimate connexion between the mind and body, and so many thousands of ways in which one alternately acts upon, and effects the other, and brings millions to an untimely grave, we see at once the propriety of not only guarding our health by temperance in eating and drinking, but more particularly by avoiding troubles of a mental character. These are generally brought upon individuals, families and neighborhoods, by the bad use of the tongue. Would you live long that you may see good days? Then keep thy tongue from evil, and thy lips from speaking guile, seek peace and pursue it. Avoid every species of iniquity that would have a tendency to blast your own or the peace of others. Avoid it as you would the poisonous exhalations of the Bohon Upas, and fly it as you would the dreadful Samiel of the Arabian desert.

SERMON II

"What man is he that desireth life and loveth many days that he may see good? Keep thy tongue from evil, and thy lips from speaking guile; depart from evil and do good, seek peace and pursue it." Psalm xxxiv:12-14.

We have shown in our last number that the truth of this text is based upon philosophy, and verified by experience and observation: that nothing is more destructive to health and longevity than to indulge in the revengeful passions of our nature; and that constant fear, grief and melancholy are also destructive to the human constitution, and withering to the dearest joys of life. We have shown that violent anger, revenge and most of the malignant passions originate from the bad use of the tongue; and that if we would live long and see good, we must give heed to our ways by following the injunctions of the text. We now propose a further discussion of this subject, addressed particularly to the young.

A single spark of fire has often wrapped a city in conflagration. Great effects not unfrequently flow from small causes. The apostle James says, see chap. iii—"Behold also the ships, which though they be so great, and are driven of fierce winds, yet they are turned about with a very small helm whithersoever the governor listeth. Even so the tongue is a little member and boasteth great things. Behold how great a matter a little fire kindleth! And the tongue is a fire, a world of iniquity; so is the tongue among our members, that it defileth the whole body, and setteth on fire the course of nature, and is set on fire of hell. For every kind of beasts and of birds, and of serpents, and of things in the sea is tamed, and hath been tamed of mankind. But the tongue can no man tame; it is an unruly member full of deadly poison." The apostle, in the above quotation, has reference to those who have so long indulged in evil speaking that it has become, as it were, an incurable habit. If any man makes a practice of slandering his neighbors, and disturbing the peace of the community, it is immaterial to what church he may belong, or what ostentatious professions he may make, he is, notwithstanding all this, destitute of christianity.

It is a painful fact that the religion of the present day is too much accommodated to the fashions and customs of the world. Let a man, for instance, use profane language, or get intoxicated, and he will readily be suspended from the communion of the church. But let him slander his neighbors, and little or no notice is taken of his conduct. And let him slander other denominations; and it becomes, as it were, a virtue; whereas the fact is that the latter, according to the book of God, is much the greatest crime. It is therefore wise to lay, in early youth, a foundation for a tranquil, virtuous and long life.

Thus you see my young friends that virtue and happiness, temperance, prosperity and longevity are inseparably connected by the Author of our being, who has made them to depend in a great measure upon our conduct. You have also seen that sin and misery, intemperance in body, and also intemperance in mind, such as evil speaking, violent anger, commotions, griefs and troubles, and a premature grave, are likewise inseparably and wisely connected.

And now, my young friends, which will you choose? If you love life and desire to see many days, let me exhort you to choose the *former*, and to drink freely out of that golden cup in which every earthly joy of unbroken felicity is mingled by the unerring hand of divine mercy; and let me warn you to reject the *latter*, for in it are mingled the bitter drugs of misery. Be temperate in eating and drinking. Be temperate in all your pursuits in life, and in all your desires. Be temperate in your conduct; and (as an able writer observes) pitch upon that course of life which is the most excellent, and habit will soon render it the most delightful. Avoid not only every word and action that may lead to discord and contention, but, as our text says, depart from evil and *do good*, seek peace, and pursue it. Let us do good to all our fellow creatures, and endeavor to overcome their hatred with love, and their evil with good.

Yes, my young friends, affectionately and solemnly would I urge you to begin early to curb your passions, and to study sweetness of disposition. It will soon become to you perfectly natural, and thus you will lay the foundation for a virtuous and tranquil old age. But, asks the youth, shall I live longer for subduing my passions and doing good, for seeking peace and pursuing it? Certainly. Our text teaches this; so does philosophy, and the scriptures generally. Jesus Christ says, "Blessed are the *meek*, for they shall inherit the earth." That is, they shall long enjoy it. "Blessed are the peace-makers for they shall be called the children of God." The fifth Commandment says, "Honor thy father and thy mother, that thy days may be long upon the land which the Lord thy God giveth thee." By honoring our parents, we are to understand a filial and submissive obedience to their precepts by not departing from that way in which with many exhortations, prayers and tears, they sought to train us up. In this case, honoring them would of course require us to walk in the paths of virtue and temperance, and to live an honest, quiet and peaceable life which would ensure the promise, and give us many days.

Not only do the scriptures promise long life to the peaceable, temperate and meek, but they on the other hand just as solemnly declare that "the wicked shall not live out half their days." This passage has occasioned much dispute among religious denominations; one affirming that every man's time is appointed in the counsels of heaven by the decree of God, who "declares the end from the beginning;" and another affirming that *it is not*, for the above passage teaches that the life of man may be shortened. But there is no occasion for dispute on this point, for they are both right, as we have seen in the course of our remarks. This passage is but the counterpart of our text. It is the decree of God that the wicked, the abandoned shall not reach the extreme of human life, because they indulge in those very crimes, which, in the constitution of things, must inevitably carry them to an early tomb. Of the truth of this we see thousands of instances in the world. And God has decreed that the meek, the peaceable shall reach the extreme of life, because they pitch upon that happy course of conduct which naturally leads to it. All that we are to understand by his *decree*, is that he has inseparably connected the *end* with the *means* by so constituting our natures, and so ordering his providence that *sin, dissipation, anger,* and *revenge* shall not only destroy happiness, but shorten life, so certain as men pursue such a wretched course. And that the opposite course of conduct shall not only communicate happiness, but protract life so certain as they engage in it.

Here then, my young friends, you may readily perceive how God punishes vice and rewards virtue. He does not do it by any abstract law, or arbitrary mode of procedure, but lie has in infinite wisdom interwoven, the whole in the very constitution of our natures, so that the wicked cannot go unpunished, nor the righteous unrewarded. To teach that man can indulge in vice, and yet escape its punishment by future repentance, is not only dangerous to the morals of society, but is a direct impeachment of the divine administration, as it must in such case, be defective. And to teach that men may live righteously and godly and yet go unrewarded, is equally dangerous to the morals of the community, as it is but discouraging them from engaging in a virtuous course of conduct. To teach that men are to be rewarded in a future world for their *goodness* here, is but in substance saying that virtue is attended with mental misery, and so far as it fails of rewarding its possessor *here*, the balance is to be made up *hereafter*. And to teach that men are to be punished in a future state for their *badness* here, is but in substance saying, that vice is attended with some mental joys, and so far as it fails of punishing its possessor *here*, the balance is to be made up *hereafter*.

It is readily granted that the righteous may suffer. But we ought ever to make a plain distinction between afflictions and punishments, for the Bible does this. It is impossible in the nature of things that punishment can exist except in connexion with guilt. Paul and Silas were cast into prison and fastened in the stocks, on account of their religion. But nothing could disturb their mental peace—their heaven-born repose. They joyfully sung psalms, and lifted up their voices in prayer to God in the calm enjoyment of a pure unsullied conscience. They suffered afflictions that were, under the government of God, to work out for their good. There were no doubt others in that prison justly suffering for their crimes. To them it was punishment.

Because the *former* were suffering *affliction*, the *latter, punishment*. The scriptures say, "Great peace have they that love thy law; and nothing shall offend them." "There is no peace, saith my God, to the wicked;" and he who says there *is*, contradicts Jehovah.

If you would, my young friends, avoid punishment, avoid sin. If you would be happy, and enjoy a long and tranquil life, follow carefully the directions of our text; for rest assured that a contrary course of conduct will not only involve you in misery and wretchedness, but bring you to a premature grave. Let us then take warning, and not become our own executioners. Let us make the most of life we may, and not turn our present existence, which is one of heaven's choicest blessings, into a curse. Let us do good in our day and generation, and render ourselves blessings to mankind, by living soberly, righteously and peaceably in the world? Let us do justly, love mercy, and walk humbly with God—visit the widow and the fatherless in their affliction, and keep ourselves unspotted from the world.

SERMON III

"And they shall drive thee from men, and thy dwelling shall be with the beasts of the field, and they shall make thee to eat grass as oxen, and seven times shall pass over thee until thou know that the Most High ruleth in the kingdom of, men, and giveth it to whomsoever he will." Daniel iv:32.

That reason, as well as revelation, teaches an overruling providence, very few deny. There must exist in nature an omnipotent and benevolent Being to keep all her works in harmony—to touch the most secret and subtle springs of the vast machinery of the universe—to regulate seed time and harvest, summer and winter, day and night; and to throw the enrapturing charms of countless variety not only over the landscape, but over all that we behold in the heavens above, or in the earth beneath. Globes roll in the paths assigned them, and by some unseen hand are wisely kept from interfering in their orbits, and disturbing each other's motions. These facts demonstrate the existence of an omniscient, omnipotent, and Benevolent Being; and every event, transpiring in the government of the world, proclaims an omnipresent Jehovah.

He not only works in the majesty of the lightning, and in the grandeur of the storm regulating and directing the whole in its sublime career, but he notices the fall of a sparrow, and numbers the very hairs of our head. Events, the most trivial in their nature, are the objects of his notice, as well as those of the most momentous character. Were not this the case, universal disorder and ruin would soon find their way into his works, break the chain of events, and reduce all, that we now admire, from its present harmony and glory, down to its general confusion and chaos. This conclusion is unavoidable, because some of the greatest events that have transpired in the world, owe their existence to something of a very trivial nature.

If God did not, in the general government of the world, direct also *small events*, then he could not be the author of those great events which flow from them. On this principle there might transpire countless events of the greatest magnitude without the direction and superintendance of Deity. The admission of *this* is but practical Atheism. It is acknowledging a God in words, but in works denying him. It alike makes *chance* the governor of the world to those who acknowledge such a God, as to those who wholly deny his existence.

In our text a presiding Deity is solemnly recognized by the prophet Daniel, and his supremacy over the affairs of men is throughout the whole chapter most strikingly set forth before the Assyrian king. He had dreamed a dream which none of the wise men of Babylon were able to interpret. Daniel was called to him; who after making known to that proud monarch his destiny involved in that dream, expostulates with him on his conduct. He did not threaten him with endless punishment in tile immortal world, but informed him that there was a God that ruled the heavens, and presided over the affairs of men; and exhorted him to forsake his iniquities. This is his language: "And whereas they commanded to leave the stump of the tree roots, thy kingdom shall be sure unto thee, after thou shalt have known that the heavens do rule. Wherefore, O king! Let my counsel be acceptable unto thee, and break off thy sins by righteousness, and thine iniquities by showing mercy to the poor, if it may be a lengthening of thy tranquillity. All this came upon the king Nebuchadnezzar. At the end of twelve months, he walked in the palace of the kingdom of Babylon. The king spake, and said, Is not this great Babylon, that I have built for the house of my kingdom, by the might of my power and for the honor of my majesty? While the word was in the king's mouth, there fell a voice from heaven, saying, O king Nebuchadnezzar! To thee it is spoken; the kingdom is departed from thee. And they shall drive thee from men, and thy dwelling shall be with the beasts of the field; they shall make thee to eat grass as oxen, and seven times shall pass over thee, until thou know that the Most High ruleth in the kingdom of men, and giveth it to whomsoever he will."

Nebuchadnezzar was the Son of Nabopolasser, and the second king of Assyria. He was Regent with his father in the Empire 607 years before the birth of our Lord, and the next year, he raised a powerful army, marched against Jerusalem, and took Jehoiakim, king of Judah, prisoner. While making preparations to carry him and his subjects into captivity, in Babylon, Jehoiakim solemnly promised submission, and begged the privilege of holding his throne under the sceptre of Nebuchadnezzar. This favor was granted, and he was permitted to remain at Jerusalem. Three years after this, he made an unsuccessful attempt to throw off the Assyrian yoke and regain his former independence. This brought on the general captivity of the Jewish nation, which lasted 70 years.

Nebuchadnezzar extended his conquests till he subjugated the Ethiopians, Arabians, Idumeans, Philistines, Syrians, Persians, Medes, Assyrians, and nearly all Asia to his sceptre. These splendid conquests, and being now king of kings, lifted up his heart with pride, that he caused a golden image to be reared on the plains of Dura. He issued a royal edict, and commanded the princes and rulers of all these nations as well as their principal subjects to assemble; and being assembled, he commanded them to fall down and worship his golden god. Daniel's companions refused to do this, and were cast into the fiery furnace.

From this circumstance he was brought to acknowledge a Supreme Being, and even issued a decree that any one who spoke amiss against the God of Shadrach, Meshach and Abednego should be cut in pieces. But as he was gazing upon the massy walls of Babylon—a work of gigantic achievement; as he was surveying, from the height of his palace, the hanging gardens and lofty towers, (an aerial world!) as he was admiring his own magnificence, by the sentence of that God whom he had glorified, he was driven from men, and in the Hebrew style of expression, is said to have eaten grass like oxen. By this we are to understand that he was suddenly seized with a disease called by the Greeks lycanthropy, and which is known among physicians at the present day by the name of hypochondria. It is a species of madness that causes persons to run into the fields and streets in the night, and sometimes to suppose themselves to have the heads of oxen, horses, dogs, or fancy themselves to be like some other animal, and doomed to fare like them. And some have imagined themselves to be made of glass. At the end of seven years Nebuchadnezzar's understanding returned to him, and he was restored to his throne and glory. He died 562 years before Christ in the 43rd year of his reign.

It is our intention to consider this text in a moral point of view, as applicable to all men of all ages, and in all conditions in life. While pursuing the various occupations to which our inclination, or fancy may lead, we are too apt to lose sight of that Being who holds our destinies in his hand; and more particularly so in seasons of prosperity, when blest with health and other sublunary enjoyments. Strange as it may seem, yet it is substantially true, that in proportion as man is successful in the accomplishment of his plans, he becomes arrogant and haughty in his feelings, and instead of acknowledging his dependence on God, and feeling the bursts of gratitude for the favors and enjoyments heaven scatters in his path, he loses sight of the benign hand that blesses him, and, like the proud Assyrian monarch, ascribes all his prosperity to his own plans, and to the effect of his own peculiar management. He surveys the lands he has purchased, the beautiful buildings he has erected, the wealth he has accumulated, and in view of these achievements of his hand, as he is floating on the full tide of prosperity, he is ready to breathe out in exultation,—"is not this great Babylon which I have built for the house of my kingdom, by the might of my power and for the honor of my majesty."

When success becomes common, man forgets his dependence on Him who rules in the armies of heaven, and over the affairs of men. It is our duty as intelligent creatures to exercise our reason in viewing things as they really are. He, who will not do this, but goes through life thoughtless, so far resigns the man, and assumes the brute. Even some, who bear the christian name, proclaim against reason, call her carnal, and prostrate her as it were at the shrine of enthusiasm. They lean upon certain frames and feelings of the animal nature. They are so far driven from men. I say it is our duty as rational intelligences to hold our station in the scale of being, and to exercise our reason in viewing things as they are. We ought candidly and solemnly to weigh the blessings of God, and consider the relation in which we stand to him as our Creator and Benefactor. Who can tell the value of existence, or number its countless joys? What a wonderful production is man! He has given us the most beautiful symmetry of parts,—has moulded our limbs with accuracy, and freely bestowed these admirable lineaments of form! He has formed the ear for sound, and awakened in its vocal chambers the flowing charms of music, the harmony of rejoicing nature, the dear voices of parents and children, and the sweet whisperings of love and friendship! He has moulded the transparent eye, bedded it in its bony socket, and on its retina painted the universe! He has bid it not only to disclose, all the varied passions of the soul, but to roll with softness and affection on the fond companion of our ways, on the countless beauties of nature, and bid it with infinite ease sweep the entire vault of heaven. He has set in motion the warm current of life that rolls through our veins, pouring nourishment, health and animation through all the channels of existence. It is he who throbs the heart, who heaves the lungs, and who bids the ten thousand complicated parts of this organized frame move on. In all this, his goodness is every moment felt, and yet we are thoughtless of these manifestations of his loving kindness. They are so common that we have ceased to prize them. When sickness and distress come upon us, it is then we learn the value of health and ease, and are often awakened to the reality that the Most High rules.

In view of the trials incident to life, we hear the Psalmist exclaim "Before I was afflicted I went astray, but now have I kept thy word." This seems to be the lamentable condition of man. When rolling in the calm tide of uninterrupted prosperity, and rejoicing in the vigor of health, he forgets there is a God, or becomes thoughtless that the heavens do rule, and begins, like the king of Babylon, to ascribe all his success to his own power, foresight and management, and is practically an atheist. But however thoughtless men may be, yet there is a God who governs the world, and will so order and direct his providence, that every one who goes counter to the principles of rectitude is *doomed, inevitably* doomed, to suffer the consequences.

There is too much practical atheism in the world. By this we mean that there are too many of those who acknowledge a God in words, that deny him in conduct. Every one, who lives upon the bounties of heaven, who enjoys the sweets of existence, and remains thoughtless of God, is practically an atheist. As saith Paul, "They profess that they know God, but in works they deny him, being abominable and disobedient, and unto every good work reprobate." He, who goes on in the ways of transgression and multiplies his iniquities, must either believe there is no God, or else conclude that he does not rule over the affairs of men; and on this ground flatters himself that he shall escape punishment. And not only so, but in opposition to the express declaration of Jehovah, he believes that he shall enjoy a degree of happiness in the indulgence of sin. All such are driven from those rational reflections and moral principles, which virtually constitute the man, and have yet to learn, "that the heavens do rule."

SERMON IV

"And they shall drive thee from men, and thy dwelling shall be with the beasts of the field, and they shall make thee to eat grass as oxen, and seven times shall pass over thee until thou know that the Most High ruleth in the kingdom of, men, and giveth it to whomsoever he will." Daniel iv:32.

Every man, who believes that the path of virtue is thorny, and that of vice is pleasurable, is not only deceived, but has not yet learned that the Most High holds the reins of government, and dispenses to his creatures their rewards and punishments. It is evident, if every man solemnly believed that a course of sin would bring upon him certain and unavoidable misery—and that every species of dishonesty would lessen his fortune in the world, he would abandon his course, and turn his feet to the testimonies of God. The transgressor is therefore deceiving himself, is resting under a strong delusion, and is yet ignorant that the Almighty rules throughout his vast dominions. Certain it is that a wicked man was never happy while remaining in that condition, and it is equally certain that no one ever yet went unpunished.

To this point we intend to invite your serious attention in this discourse. The expression in our text, "till thou know that the Most High ruleth in the kingdom of men," does not only imply a knowledge of the existence of a Supreme Intelligence, who governs the world, but an obedience to the moral laws of his empire. On this proposition we purpose to offer a few rational, and not only rational, but irresistible arguments. We will first notice the condition of those who are guilty of heinous crimes, and then come down to the common walks of life, and bestow a few remarks on those who are indifferent about their condition, and only guard their conduct so far as comports with the customs and manners of that portion of the community, who have no higher principle of action than to be considered respectable among men.

Though we come before the public to defend the doctrines of Christ, yet, my friends, you will bear in mind that it is also our duty to enforce his precepts, and exhort to the obedience of the gospel. That we should point out the road of sin, error and misery, and also endeavor to throw the light of heavenly truth on the pathway of human life.

We will begin with the murderer, who wantonly embrues his hands in the blood of his fellow. So far as he has violated the laws of his country, he is a subject for public execution, and has nothing to hope for, at the tribunal of human justice. His misery, whether it arise from the contemplation of an ignominious death, from the fear of detection, or from the consciousness of having violated the moral principles of his nature, is alike insupportable, as well as indescribable.

Is he detected? Shut out from the world and confined in his loathsome cell, he is left to his own reflections, and to all the horrors of the gathering storm. But even admitting that he should escape detection, and be left to his own meditations on his deed of blood, he would, like Cain, breathe out in agony of soul, "my punishment is greater than I can bear!" He might, indeed, mingle with the busy throng—he might even smile, and wear a face of pleasure, but behind this mantled mask he would conceal a heart of pain. He might, indeed, gaze upon the landscape, listen to the songs of the grove, and contemplate the glories of nature, but the charm, that once gave him ecstatic delight and solid joy, is vanished from his sight; and all, that once was fair and lovely, wears the frown of darkness and indignation. He gazes upon little children, and hears their artless and innocent prattle, reflects what he once was, and every joy, that sparkles in their eyes, sends a dagger to his heart. The rustling of a leaf strikes him with terror and alarm, and every passing breeze bears to his tormented soul the groans of the dying man, and conscience forces him to listen to the heart-rending tale of wo. Fain would he fly from himself, and enjoy one hour's repose; but alas! That God, who rules in the kingdom of men, has written a law in his heart, where he reads and feels his condemnation, and where conscience sits on the judgment seat, constantly holds him arraigned at her tribunal, and fans up in his bosom the burning flames of hell! He may lie down on his pillow, but spectres haunt his brain; and awake, asleep, at home, abroad, he finds that he has rendered his own existence a curse. He lives in misery, and in darkness expires.

Let us next notice the thief, who plunders our property. His crime is of less magnitude than the above, but his guilt is in proportion. No one by such means has ever enriched himself. He, who obtains property by dishonorable means, is ignorant of its value, and will dishonorably spend it. He has forgotten that God governs the world. Our state-prisons and penitentiaries not only (so far as human laws are concerned) reveal his fate, but speak his woes. But suppose he escape detection, and is only exposed to the naked and fearful grandeur of that law which God has written in the heart. He hears its thunders, and he feels its fires. He his taken from some fellow being his hard earnings; and sees him and perhaps his children mourning their misfortune and suffering the miseries of adversity. Guilt takes possession of his soul, and misery, which the hand of time cannot extinguish, rolls its dark waves of damnation upon him, and drowns his dearest joys, while poverty marks him for her own.

God has so constituted his plans in the government of the world that the plunderer cannot prosper. Inward horrors and fears of detection abstract his mind from the proper duties of life, so that misfortune and defeat find their way into his plans, which might otherwise by calm deliberation have succeeded, and disappointment and misery, satiety and disgust, and all the evils that are the offspring of his iniquity, commingling in a thousand ways, render his existence wretched. Relying upon dishonesty for support, he becomes but a midnight beggar. His slumbers are haunted by frightful dreams; and fear of detection, prisons and dungeons are torturing his imagination and incessantly sporting with his broken peace. He is a stranger to those solid joys arising from the practice of virtue, is doomed to encounter all the miseries that attend his ill-chosen career, and to drink every drug of wormwood and gall that heaven has mingled in the cup of dishonor. He lives a nuisance and pest to society, and dies covered with infamy.

In all this we shall see the truth of our text exemplified, that God rules in the kingdom of men, and brings punishment, not only upon a haughty monarch seated on the throne of nations, but upon every transgressor however obscure may be his condition in the walks of private life. The sovereign decree of his empire is—"THOUGH HAND JOIN IN HAND, YET SHALL THE WICKED NOT GO UNPUNISHED."

But we take our leave of flagitious crimes and proceed to notice men in the common walks of life. Every man who makes riches, or public honors the chief end of all his pursuits, and gives all his attention to the attainment of his object, and over-reaches in bargains whenever an opportunity offers, or sets various prices on his merchandise, according to the person with whom he deals—such a man will never feel himself filled with riches, nor satisfied with honors. The reasons are obvious. He commences his career under the impression that happiness, contentment and all the rational enjoyments of life consist in wealth, and in human greatness. He soon finds himself in possession of as large a fortune as he first supposed would make him happy. But his desires for more, having imperceptibly expanded, he finds within an increased restlessness, and even greater desires for *more* than when he first set out. He still believes, according to his original impression, that happiness lies in gold; and that the only reason why he has not obtained those solid joys in possession which he first anticipated, is because he still needs more. But though wealth may flow upon him in oceans, his cravings for more will ever swell beyond what earth can give, and leave him a more wretched being than he was at the commencement of his course. Here is his loss—here is his punishment. God has not placed happiness in wealth. *"A competence is all we can enjoy, O, be content where heaven can give no more."*

Or let him rise to that station of honor, which he now believes will satisfy him, and his ambition would aspire to one more exalted. Let him govern one kingdom, and he would desire to subjugate another till the whole world bowed to his nod. And were every star an inhabited world, and did he possess means to invade them, his ambition would continue to soar till he ruled the universe, and were there no object left to which he might still direct his ambition and continue to soar, he would set down in despair, and, like Alexander the Great, weep and sigh for more worlds to conquer.

All this restlessness and misery arise from false notions of: happiness—from not realizing that the Most High rules in the kingdom of men—and from a want of confidence in his word, which points the rich and the poor alike to that noble path of virtue and religion, where true happiness and unbroken peace forever reign. By men embracing virtue, and in their feelings and actions ever acknowledging the supremacy of Jehovah, inevitably leads to happiness and contentment. But in doing this we are not to deprive ourselves of the enjoyment of honest gotten wealth, nor of the rational pursuits and interchanges of social and domestic life. Religion was not given to deprive us of the common comforts and conveniences of life, but to sweeten them. Our Redeemer says, "seek first the kingdom of God and his righteousness; and all these things shall be added unto you." Sin and misery in this world are inseparable: so are righteousness and happiness. If they are not, then it remains for the advocates for a future retribution to show how men are to be sufficiently rewarded and punished in the future world.

There is my friends no solid happiness, no permanent satisfaction only in the contemplation that God governs the world, and in the practice of pure and rational piety. This you may know by studying your own bosom. Have any of you thus far spent your days in striving to find perfect bliss in the various pursuits of life? Have you aspired to one object, abandoned it, and taken up another? If so, can you say that you have found the happiness you anticipated, and so earnestly sought? No! What is the reason? There is one thing needful. Whatever may be your pursuit, if you are thoughtless that God governs the world, and if instead of rendering him the homage of a grateful heart, you blaspheme his name, or are selfish and regardless of the happiness of your fellow creatures, you must, according to the established laws of his empire, remain in that same restless and dissatisfied condition till you know by experience that the heavens do rule—till you bow to the sublime requirements of his word. *That dissatisfaction* varied according to the condition of moral character is the punishment God sends upon us for our indifference. From this indifference we may rise to that unquenchable thirst for riches, already noticed, and our sufferings will receive new accessions according to our moral light. And from this we may rise to a desire for honour and power, till we are hurried on by ambition to conquest and slaughter where we are doomed to suffer all the miseries a Buonaparte endured. From this we may rise to dishonour, fraud and theft; and as we rise in crime, our miseries increase in degree, till we imbrue our hands in innocent blood, and thus render our bosoms a hell and our very existence a burthen.

Every man is in a condition of uneasiness, suffering, guilt, hardness of heart and blindness of mind exactly in proportion to his moral conduct. Let us then be wise;—and if we desire happiness, let us seek it in that course where the unerring word of God assures us it can alone be found. Let us acknowledge "that the heavens do rule," and rest assured that He, who notices the fall of a sparrow, will not wink at our evil doings.

SERMON V

"For what if some did not believe, shall their unbelief make the faith of God without effect? God forbid; yea let God be true, but every man a liar." Romans iii:3, 4.

The doctrine of salvation by Jesus Christ, is worthy the solemn consideration of all men. It is this, that rendered a revelation necessary. It is this that kindled the flame of transport in celestial bosoms, and raised that triumphant song, "glory to God in the highest, on earth peace, good will towards men." Salvation is the doctrine of the Bible, and ought ever to be the theme of the pulpit. Salvation is the oracle of heaven around which all denominations assemble, receive their instructions, and believe according to the force of evidence.

Prefaced with these remarks, we will now proceed to state what we conceive to be the *law and gospel*—point out the distinction between them, and defend the gospel doctrine of salvation of faith.

The law was a conditional covenant between God and man. It was predicated on works. Under this covenant, if a man were strictly moral in his external deportment—if he lived up to its letter, he was considered righteous. This covenant was imperfect, because it could be kept externally without reaching the heart. They could exclaim like the young man, who came to Jesus—"all these things have I kept from my youth up," and still lack the one great point, charity. Therefore by the deeds of the law no flesh could be justified in the sight of God. The law, being temporary in its nature, had nothing to do with eternal things.

Paul says, "sin is the transgression of the law. Where there is no law there is not the knowledge of sin." From this it appears that sin, being a transgression of that law, which was given us for the regulation of our conduct in this life, can receive no punishment in the future world. If sin should be committed in the future state, then in the future state it would be punished. The same argument will apply to our obedience to the law, which can receive, for the same reason, no reward in that world. "No flesh shall be justified by the deeds of the law." "Eternal life is the gift of God." If so, then it cannot be "of works, lest any man should boast." God, being infinite in wisdom, could not have failed to enact a law so perfect, and so exactly adapted to the nature of man, that *obedience* would render him a rich reward, and *disobedience* a condign punishment. The wise man says that "the righteous shall be recompensed in the earth; much more the wicked and the sinner."

We now turn to the spirit of the law.—"To love the Lord thy God with all thy heart, and thy neighbor as thyself is the fulfillment of the law;" and if we are not to be saved by the law, then our *love* to God and each other cannot save us; for that is the law. By what then are we to be saved? Answer: by the gospel, which is God's love manifested to his creatures. The conclusion then is that we are not to be saved by our *love* to God, but by God's *love* to us. This, I presume, no one will dispute. Here then we discern the difference between the law and the gospel. God's love is the *cause* of salvation—human love is the *effect*. "Herein (says John) is love; not that we loved God, but that he loved us." "We love him *because* he *first* loved us." How many did he love? He so loved the world who were dead in trespasses and sins, that he freely delivered up his Son for us all—he by the grace of God tasted death for every man. This is the gospel-love that God commendeth towards us, and the love that will finally save us.

Many persons contend that we must love God and do certain duties, or we cannot be saved. This is preaching ourselves. It is preaching the love of man as the cause of his salvation, instead of the love of God. And while thus preaching, they will perhaps at the same time tell the sinner that God is his enemy. But will the sinner's love make God his friend—will it cause his Creator to love him? No; right the reverse of this is the doctrine of Christ. "We love God because he first loved us." If we deny God's *first* love to the sinner, we then destroy the very *cause* by which *alone* the sinner can be made to love God. If we make men believe that God is their enemy and hates them, then we use all the means in our power to drive them from the bosom of their Father, and keep them in darkness and sin.

The sinner, in this situation, can never be made to serve God, only by being driven to it by terror, the same as some wretched slave is made to cower and submit in fear and dread to some revengeful tyrant. But this is not the service God requires. He requires a service which is delightful, and in which his creature feels an abundant reward. We grant that men, under the first covenant, were called upon to fear God. The reason of this obvious, when we reflect that God had covenanted to bestow certain blessings upon them, providing they would do their duty. If they failed, then he would execute the temporal judgments upon them, which the law points out, and threatens. Under this covenant men had just as much reason to fear, as they were liable to transgress it.

But when an angel announced the dawn of a better covenant; he said "fear not, for behold I bring you glad tidings of great joy." In this is nothing to be feared. All the fear lies in the first, and thunders out to ever sinner, "cursed is every one that continueth not in all things written in the law to do them?" But John, speaking in view of the second covenant, says, "there is no fear in love; but perfect love casteth out fear, because fear hath torment. He that feareth is not made perfect in love." The *first* covenant is founded on works, and is *conditional*;—but the *second* is founded on the immutable promise of

God, and is *unconditional*. In the law, we are commanded *to do* according to the reasonableness of its requirements; but in the gospel we are exhorted *to believe* in view of evidence and fact. And as no man can believe, or disbelieve what he pleases, therefore conditions are excluded.

What is the meaning of gospel? It is good tidings of great joy. It is life and immortality brought to light at the appearing of our Lord and Saviour, Jesus Christ, who has abolished death by giving us the assurance of a resurrection from corruption to incorruption and glory. It is news. In view of news, what is the first thing necessary? Answer, *belief*. It is impossible to work news; therefore the gospel is not of works. In the law, the first requirement is *to do*;—but in the gospel the first requirement is *to believe*. The law-covenant is therefore temporary, fallible and uncertain; but the gospel-covenant is eternal, infallible, and in all things well ordered and sure. The *first* rests on the obedience of the creature, but the *second* on the promises of Jehovah. Paul therefore calls it a better covenant established upon *better* promises.

Perhaps someone may feel disposed to ask—whether faith is all that is necessary? We reply that it is the cause which produces its effect. Paul answers this question thus—"We conclude that a man is justified by faith without the deeds of the law, Do we then make void the law through faith? God forbid; yea we establish the law." Here let the question be asked;—how do we establish the law by *faith*? Answer, "Faith will have its perfect work." But what is that perfect work, which faith produces? Ans. Faith works love in the soul; and if we love God, we will keep his commandments. And *faith, love* and *keeping* the commandments are the three exercises, that form the christian character. Faith is the foundation; works are not. We cannot begin to build on works. Instead of being the *first*, they are the *last* christian grace. They are the visible *effects* of an inward, living faith.

Faith and faith *only* is the seed rooted and grounded in the truth, and (to use a Bible figure) it becometh a tree, and produces all the fruits of the spirit-love, joy, meekness, temperance, long-suffering, forbearance. This is what the apostle calls the "righteousness of faith" in contradistinction to "the righteousness of the law," produced by fear. Paul compares faith to a good olive tree. "The Jews through unbelief were broken off," and "thou (the Gentile) standest by faith." Jesus says; "if ye have faith as a grain of mustard-seed, ye shall say unto this mountain, remove hence to yonder place, and it shall remove." Here, in parable, faith is represented as removing mountains of sin. He further says—"Thy *faith* hath made thee whole";—not thy works. Paul exclaims, "Faith works by love, purifies the heart and overcomes the world." John says, "and this is the victory that overcometh the world even our faith."

It is a certain fact, that none of these salutary effects are ascribed to human works. The apostles in no instance say, that *works* purify the heart, or overcome the world—or that this is the victory, even your *works*; The whole is ascribed to *faith*; because that is the living tree on which the good fruits grow. Works are, in scripture, called fruits. "By their *fruits* ye shall know them"—that is by their *works*. "A good tree cannot bring forth evil *fruit*." To carry out this figure, we would remark that, fruit can have no existence till the tree is first produced. Therefore in a gospel sense, no good works, acceptable to God, can be produced without a true and living faith. The apostle declares, "without faith it is impossible to please God." The gospel being good tidings, or news, are you satisfied that thing necessary? I presume all denominations will assent to the fact, that faith is the first religious exercise of the creature. We shall then obey the command of the apostle, and "contend earnestly for the faith once delivered to the saints."

But asks the reader, what matter is it which is first in order, whether *love, faith* or *works*? I reply that it is a matter of vast importance, and without understanding this fact, we cannot come to the knowledge of the truth, even though we should be ever learning. If these three christian graces *faith, love* and *works*, are preached in a confused and mixed manner, we cannot arrive at a true understanding of a gospel salvation, neither can we tell the difference between law and gospel. The law is of works, and the gospel is of faith. And no man can fulfill the spirit of the law without faith in the gospel. When the sinner exercises faith in the love and goodness of God in freely giving him eternal life, which infinitely transcends all other blessings—that moment faith works love in his heart, and causes him to rejoice with joy unspeakable and full of glory. He then loves God because God first loved him. And when the sinner loves God, he is passed from death unto life, and that love is the fulfillment of the law.

We are now led to see the consistency of faith being the first step. It is the very *cause* that produces *love* to God, and *love* induces us to keep the commandments. "Faith works by love," and "if ye love me," says Jesus, "ye will keep my commandments."

We will now introduce an example, which will plainly show the distinction between the law and gospel and in what manner they affect the sinner. Suppose a king sentences six of his subjects to imprisonment during life, and commands them to spend their days in hard labor. They are put in confinement, refuse to obey his commands— refuse to labor, and in the midst of their miseries curse his name. They are now in disobedience under the condemnation of the law.

The king says to his only Son, I love those subjects and I covenant with you to set them free in three years. The Son says, Father I delight to do thy will.

Let me go and reveal to them, the glad tidings of this covenant promise. The king answers—my Son, in the fullness of time I will send you. Let them remain, one year, under the law. But says the Son, they are now transgressing your law, and need instruction. The king replies, I will send my servant to enforce that law. Let him go and inform the prisoners, that I am angry with them for their conduct; and if they will obey my commands, and labor faithfully, they shall have excellent food and good clothing as a reward. But if they will not comply, they shall be chained, and kept on bread and water as a punishment for their disobedience.

The servant goes and delivers to them this message. Three of those subjects, for fear of the punishment and in *hope* of the reward, obey the king, and outwardly respect his commands, but perhaps have little, or no love for him. (Here we see the righteousness of the law which is not acceptable to God.) They accordingly receive, day by day, the promised reward. But the other three prisoners despise these conditions and refuse to obey. They are chained, fed on bread and water, and meet their deserts.

Here, then, are six prisoners laboring under the law, and groaning in bondage with no hopes of deliverance. The law knows of no deliverance —no redemption. It simply serves as a school master to teach them the difference between right and wrong—to teach them the will of the king, and thus prepare them to receive a better covenant, which is to be revealed to them by the king's Son. But under the covenant they now are, they have no motives to prompt them to obedience, but the *fear* of punishment and the *hope* of reward. In our next, this will be fully illustrated.

SERMON VI

"For what if some did not believe, shall their unbelief make the faith of God without effect? God forbid; yea let God be true, but every man a liar." Romans iii:3, 4.

We resume the argument, in this discourse, concerning those prisoners brought forward in our last. We left them in bondage under the sentence of the law with no hopes of deliverance. The first year rolls away. The king says, my son, the time has come—go, and reveal my love to the prisoners by bringing the promise of their redemption to light. The son flies on wings of love, enters the prison and exclaims—I bring you good tidings of great joy. My father, the king, is your friend. He loves you; and that love has induced him to proclaim your liberation as a free gift. He has promised (and he cannot lie) that in two years from this day you shall be free. This covenant, so far as concerns its fulfillment, is unconditional. Believe, and you will be saved, by faith in the promise, from your present fears, and condemnation under the law.

Those stubborn prisoners see a sufficiency of evidence to believe the promise. They exercise unshaken faith in this second covenant between the father and son. This faith works by love in their hearts, and purifies them from disobedience. Their souls melt in view of the love and goodness of the king revealed to them by his son. In fine, they love him because he first loved them. They are now saved by faith in his promise from not only all their miseries and sorrows, but from their disobedience, and look forward with joy to the day of redemption. Here we perceive the "*righteousness of faith*," which far exceeds the "*righteousness of the law.*" They now delight to obey the king because they are under the influence of love.

Here let the question be asked—are these three men to be let out of prison at the appointed time because they believe the promise, or love and obey the king? They are not. Their redemption depended on the truth and faithfulness of the king's promise which he made to his son, and that promise would have been fulfilled, even if it had not been revealed to them till the day of their deliverance. They are not to be set free as a reward for their *faith, love and obedience*. They have great peace and joy in believing that promise. They are in the happy enjoyment of a salvation by faith, and that is all the reward they deserve, or have reason to expect. We here perceive that these three men are made to establish the law of their king by faith in the good news he sent them by his son, which is to them a gospel. We now see the propriety of the apostle's language—"We conclude that a man is justified by faith without the deeds of the law. Do we then make void the law through faith? God forbid; yea we establish the law." We also perceive that these three men are not to be liberated from prison because they believe the promise, or love and obey the king. But on the contrary it is the king's love and promise to them which sets them free.

Let us now notice the other three prisoners. One says I do not believe that we shall ever be released from prison. It is too good news to be true. Well, shall his unbelief make the king's promise of none effect? The king forbid; yea let the king be true, but that man a liar. But let it be remembered that he cannot be proved a liar unless he is liberated. Would you now go and tell that man—sir, because you will not *believe*, you shall never come forth from prison? But do you not perceive that by so doing you would give the king the lie? It would be saying that his promise was good for nothing unless the man would believe it. It would be contending that the unbelief of this prisoner will make the king's promise of none effect.

The other two prisoners exclaim—we believe this *second* covenant, but it must bear some resemblance to the first which is conditional. We believe that we shall get out of this prison if we continue to serve the king as, we have heretofore, by keeping his commandments.— Here are two men trusting in the *first covenant* for deliverance. They are trusting in the law. They are depending on their own *love and faithfulness* to the king for redemption, and not on the king's *love, promise and faithfulness* to them. Here then we see the righteousness of the law in those two prisoners; in another we see the effect of unbelief; and in those three who remained disobedient under the first covenant, we see the righteousness which is of faith when they heard the glad tidings of redemption in the second covenant.

At length the day of their redemption dawns. They are all brought to the knowledge of the truth. Those three prisoners, who were saved by faith in the promise during those two years of suspense, now find their faith lost in certainty. Their salvation, by faith has come to an end. And so has the unbelief, condemnation and doubtings of the other three prisoners. In one word—the *belief and unbelief* of the six are lost in knowledge, and they burst out in songs of deliverance So we perceive that a salvation by faith, and a condemnation in unbelief can last no longer than till we come to the knowledge of the truth.

Let us now apply this to the scriptures. Man sinned, and not only involved himself in guilt and misery, but was sentenced to that very death with which God threatened him—"Dust thou art and unto dust shalt thou return." Here was the end of the first covenant, and the termination of all the miseries of life. It is evident from revelation as well as reason that man at death drops to a state of insensibility, and knows no more till he is made alive in Christ, who is himself the second covenant. The language of scripture is, the dead know not any thing—they sleep—and the apostle (in 1 Cor. xv Chap.) reasons that if there be no resurrection, then there will be no future existence— that they which are fallen asleep in Christ are perished—that preaching was vain—faith was also vain, and that the christians were yet in their sins. On such language as this, I can put no other construction than that the resurrection is our salvation and eternal life, our deliverance from sin and imperfection. Under the first covenant the resurrection in Christ was not revealed to the human family, and they remained of course under the sentence of condemnation with no hopes of a future existence. "By the offense of one judgment came upon all men to condemnation." Obedience to the law was enforced by threatenings on the one hand, and promises of temporal rewards on the other, which were communicated to the fathers by the prophets.

But God has in these latter days spoken unto us by his Son, and through him revealed the second covenant in which he "gave him the heathen for an inheritance, and the utter most parts of the earth for a possession," and declared him to be the resurrection and life of the world. If in the divine counsels no Christ had been provided, the human family it appears would have remained in eternal slumber. They would have known but one covenant, which would have rewarded and punished them according to their deeds, and consigned them to the regions of the dead. "But since by man came death, by man came also the resurrection of the dead."

God saw fit to keep the human family for four thousand years under the first covenant, without the knowledge of eternal life through the resurrection of the dead. But it was, at length, "made manifest by the appearing of our Saviour Jesus Christ, who hath abolished death, and brought life and immortality to light through the gospel." Yes, he first brought it to light, and through his apostle declared "In hope of eternal life which God that cannot lie promised before the world began, but hath in due time manifested his word through preaching." This promise of eternal life, all men are called upon to believe. The moment they believe, they are saved by faith, and are at peace; and they that doubt are damned—they are already under condemnation. But shall their unbelief make God's promise of eternal life of none effect? God forbid; yea let God be true but every man a liar. "For he hath concluded them all in unbelief that he might have mercy upon all."

We have now noticed the two covenants—the *law and gospel*—have pointed out the distinction between them—shown that all *conditions* are confined to the law, and that the gospel is *unconditional*, and justly requires our faith and confidence. We will now bring to view the scripture doctrine of salvation by faith, and show that divine truth must have an existence before we can be called upon to believe.

All scripture is given by inspiration of God and is based upon eternal and unchanging truth. Truth is one of the attributes of Jehovah and the unshaken pillar that supports the throne of eternity. In truth and righteousness he governs the world, and by an omnipotent arm wields the destinies of men. Truth is the sun of divine revelation pouring its beams on intelligent creation and calling upon all men to believe. If a man assert that which does exist, it is a truth; but if he assert that which does not exist, it is a falsehood. Whatever has an existence in the compass of reality is a truth to be believed, and whatever has no such existence is a falsehood not to be believed. It is beyond the power of man to create one solitary divine truth. All that he can do is to declare the existence of that which may be hidden from others, or relate some circumstances respecting that which does absolutely exist. An absolute truth must, therefore, be presented to the understandings of men before they can be called upon to believe it, or before they can be called believers for embracing it, or *unbelievers* for rejecting it. No man can be an unbeliever for rejecting that which does not exist.

We now commence plain argument by using great plainness of speech. In preaching the gospel of Jesus Christ truth must be the foundation. If then truth must exist before men can be called upon to believe, the question arises what is that truth which the second covenant reveals for the belief of mankind? Answer, it is the record God hath given of his Son. But what is the *record*? Let John answer—"this is the record, God hath given us *eternal life*, and this life is in his Son." It then follows that we are to believe that God has given us eternal life in his Son before the world began, and unchangeably promised it. Paul says—"In hope of eternal life which God that cannot lie promised before the world began." If we believe the record, we are in the scriptures recognized as *believers* and are saved by faith, and will of course exhibit in our life and conversation the righteousness of faith.

The great error of any who read the Bible, consists in supposing there is but one salvation. But there are two. The *first* is a special salvation by belief in the promise, and the second is our eternal salvation beyond the grave, where we shall be brought to the knowledge of the truth involved in the promise, and to *know* shall be life eternal. Faith shall then be lost in certainty. Now if we disbelieve the record will that make it false? No; our unbelief cannot alter the fact. Let the record then be proclaimed to every creature—saying God has promised and given you eternal life in Christ before the world began, and calls upon all to believe it. But suppose they should all reject it saying we do not believe one word of it, would their *unbelief* make the promise or record false? No. Would not then the record prove true? It would. Then the whole world would, of course, receive that eternal life which is promised and given them in Christ. No, says the objector, they will not believe. But can their unbelief make God's promise of none effect? Can it put that truth out of existence and make it a falsehood? We would ask the objector, what will they not believe? Answer; they will not believe that God has given them eternal life in his Son. Very well,—then the whole amount of the objection is that God has given them eternal life in Christ, but they will not believe it, and because they will not believe it, they never shall obtain it! Then we must contend (if they never obtain it) that it was never given to them, and if not given, then the record is false; because the record declares that God has given them eternal life in his Son. It then follows that their unbelief can make the faithfulness of God without effect by rendering the word, he has given, false.

But says the objector it ought to be stated conditionally as follows— God first calls upon men to believe, and if they will believe, then Christ will become their Saviour, and then they will receive eternal life in him and not before. But does not the objector see that he has stated no fact for them to believe in order to make Christ their Saviour? I ask what does God call upon them to believe? There must be some truth presented before men can be called upon to believe. God calls upon men to believe, what—That Christ is their Saviour? But you said he was not their Saviour till after they believed. It then follows, according to the objector's statement, that he is not the Saviour of unbelievers. Now do you not perceive that if you should call upon them to believe that he was their Saviour, you would call upon them to believe a lie—that you would call upon them to believe what did not exist? And what does not exist cannot be true. Grant says the objector that he is the Saviour of the world, still as many as do not believe in him shall never be saved. But how can he be the Saviour of a man, he never saves? Two individuals are drowning in the water; you exert all your power to save them, but fail. Can you call yourself the saviour of those two men from temporal death? Impossible. In order for Christ to be called the Saviour of the world, he must save the world; otherwise there is not a shadow of propriety in giving him that name. And John says "We have seen and do testify that the Father sent the Son to be the Saviour of the world."—"We know, indeed, that this is the Messiah the Saviour of the world."

In our next, we will conclude this subject, and trust we shall do it to the satisfaction of our readers.

SERMON VII

"For what if some did not believe, shall their unbelief make the faith of God without effect? God forbid; yea let God be true, but every man a liar." Romans iii:3, 4.

We now resume the argument in reference to Christ the Saviour of men, as we proposed in our last. We here inquire of the objector—do you then grant that he is the Saviour of all men—the Saviour of the world as the scriptures declare? If so, we assure you that, he will save the number of whom he is declared to be the Saviour. But, replies the objector, he is not the Saviour of any man till he believes. We ask— till he believes what? Why, replies the objector, till he believes that Christ is his Saviour—if he believes so, it will be so. Let us understand this—you say *he is not* the Saviour of an unbeliever, still he must believe that he is, and that will make him so. Then he must first believe a lie and that will create a truth. This is (as Paul says) "turning the truth of God into a lie." But let us notice the record. "This is the record, God hath given us eternal life, and this life is in his Son." Do you grant, that God has given eternal life in Christ to every man? No, says the objector. Very well, then they cannot be called upon to believe it. Finally, says the objector, grant that he has. This being granted, we would ask, whether they will not come in possession of it, if God's promise stands? Certainly. But, replies the objector, it is not theirs, till they believe. Then the record is not true till they believe it; because, on this principle, they must first believe, that they have eternal life in Christ before it exists, and believing this lie will create it.

But, replies the objector, it is impossible that any man has eternal life given him in Christ, till he believes. We then ask, what truth do you wish him to believe, so that he may obtain this eternal life? The fact is, there is none. He must believe *this truth*, itself because it is the record, but this, you have taken from him. You cannot call upon a man to believe, till you admit the existence of that very truth you wish him to believe. In order fully to expose the inconsistency of this conditional salvation, we will introduce an example. Suppose a father tell his servant, I have a son in London, nineteen years of age, who is in poverty and distress. I have given him in my will five thousand dollars, and I promise that it shall be put into his possession in two years. It is recorded and that record is true. Go my servant, and proclaim to him glad tidings of great joy, and call upon him to believe, so that he may enjoy a salvation by faith during those two years of suspense, and be made happy even amidst his wants by looking forward to when it shall be put into his possession.

The servant sets out on his mission, and believes that he understands his errand. Being arrived, he addresses him as follows—Son, your father is very rich, and he has not willed you five thousand dollars, nor given it to you on record; and he never will, unless you *first believe* that he has. But, replies the son, according to your message, if I should believe that he has given me five thousand dollars, I should believe a lie. Let my father give the money, deposit it in some bank; send me evidence of the fact, and with joy I will believe him. Well replies the servant you are a disobedient, stubborn unbeliever! Because, if you would only believe so, it would be so, and you would have the money in two years.

You perceive (dear reader) that this servant has presented no truth for this son to believe. He wishes to give this son the impression that the obtaining of this fortune depends on his *believing*, and not on the *testament record, and faithfulness* of his father. In fact, he denies the existence of the father's *will*, and the *record*, and requires the son to believe a lie so as to create the truth. The servant does not understand his message, and the son does not know on what certainty to rest for the money.

In the same manner we are called upon to secure an *interest*—an eternal life in the Saviour. They will not admit its existence till we believe. Then *belief* must create it. But may we spend our last breath in convincing poor sinners that it is already secured in Christ for them, so that they may believe, and live by faith on the son of God.

This father sends another messenger. He tells this son of the goodness of his father, and that he has *willed* him five thousand dollars, that the *will* is put on record, and that this fortune will be put into his possession in two years. The son does not believe it. Now he is an unbeliever. But does his unbelief alter the truth of the *will* or of the record. No. The certainty, of his obtaining the money, rests on the faithfulness of his kind parent. This servant perseveres, uses convincing arguments and the son at length believes he is saved by faith from all his miseries, and he rejoices with joy unspeakable. But his *believing* does not make the record any more true than it was before he believed it. It simply alters his present condition by kindling in his bosom the joys arising from faith and anticipation.— We have now answered the objections that would naturally be brought forward by those who believe that our eternal salvation is predicated on conditions. As *works* are not the requirements of the gospel only so far as they flow from faith in the truth, and as *faith* must precede works, therefore the truth of our eternal life in Christ, must exist previous to our believing. Consequently all conditions are excluded from the gospel covenant.

We will now meet the objector on the doctrine of election and reprobation, the substance of which is as follows—After man fell, God was pleased to provide a Saviour for a part of the human family. That elect number he chose in Christ before the foundation of the world, gave them eternal life in him, and for them only he tasted death. The gospel is now to be preached to the whole world, and as long as they reject it, they are unbelievers. But the elect shall sooner, or later, all be brought to believe.

We will examine the foundation on which this statement rests. To bring it clearly before you, we will take an example. Suppose there is a congregation of one hundred persons. Fifty of them were elected to everlasting life before the foundation of the world—were secured by a Saviour, and the rest were reprobated to endless wo. For them no Saviour was designed, and no eternal life ever has, or ever will be given them in him. Suppose a sermon is preached to those one hundred; and the fifty, who are elected, believe the record of their eternal life, are brought to the obedience of faith, while the other fifty remain unmoved. The preacher turns upon them and pronounces them *unbelievers*. But In what sense are they unbelievers? There has been no truth presented to them, which they disbelieve. Must they believe that Christ is their Saviour, or that they have an eternal life in him? But they would in such case believe a lie. If they believed right the reverse of the elect,—*believed* that God was their enemy and that Christ was not their Saviour, they would be *believers*. But if they believed what the fifty converts did, they would be *unbelievers*. We here repeat one premise laid down in our last discourse—viz. In order for any man to be styled a *believer or unbeliever*, there must first be presented some truth for him to embrace or reject.

Now either God has given us eternal life in Christ before the world began, or he has not. If he has, then we are *unbelievers* if we reject it. If he has not given it, and should we still believe that he has, we would then believe a lie. But neither our *belief, or unbelief* can ever alter the fact.

God has "chosen us in Christ before the foundation of the world that we should be holy and without blame before him in love; having predestinated us unto the adoption of children by Jesus Christ to himself according to the good pleasure of his will." * * * "Having made known unto us the mystery of his will according to his good pleasure which he hath purposed in himself; that in the dispensation of the fullness of times, he might gather together, in one, all things in Christ, both which are in heaven and which are on earth, even in him." Some apply the above to the elect. But it embraces all things in heaven and earth, which are to be gathered together in Christ, and be new creatures. In addition to this we will introduce two more passages "Who hath saved us, and called us with a holy calling, not according to our works, but according to his own purpose and grace which was given us in Christ Jesus before the world began." "In hope of eternal life, which God, that cannot lie, promised before the world began." In these scriptures we are assured *first*, that God chose us in Christ, before the foundation of the world—*second*, that he saved us according to his own purpose and grace before the world began, and *third* that he promised eternal life before the world began. These things being embraced in his original plan, and purpose, their performance is therefore certain as that the whole plan of God will be carried unto execution.

There is, in my humble opinion, a strange inconsistency in the common doctrine. They contend that on account of the transgression of our first parent, all mankind were fallen creatures and even came into existence totally depraved. To show the justice of God in the constitution of our nature, they contend that Adam was our covenant head, and had he maintained his original purity, we would also have stood perfect in holiness, and no one would have had any reason to complain. Now since Adam has fallen, and involved us in ruin, it is equally just in God that we should share the fate of our covenant head in the one instance as in the other. But if we make use of this same argument in relation to Christ, the second Adam—if we contend that he was the covenant head of every man, that the covenant was not made for *this*, but for the *future* world—that this covenant of grace being made between the Father and the Son, was to stand independent of man— that eternal life was promised and given us in him before the world began—that as our covenant head, he resisted all temptations, and perfectly fulfilled the law—that he died, and appeared alive beyond the tomb free from temptation, and in a holy and immortal constitution. If we contend for this, making use of their own arguments, saying that it is just as rational that we should appear in the image of Christ in the future world as that we should come into this world in the image of Adam, they will pronounce the argument so far as applicable to Adam, *sound logic*, but so far as this same argument of theirs is applied by Universalists to Christ, they pronounce it perfect jargon.

But, says the objector, there is one point you have not settled, and I will here rest the whole of my argument upon it. It is this—God has, in no instance, promised eternal to *unbelievers*; and unless you can prove that the promise does extend to them, your arguments must fall like rottenness to the ground. We have certainly proved this, and to attend to the objector's request would but be, in some measure, going over the ground already occupied. We will, however, just touch this point again. We will introduce the following words of Paul to Titus. "In hope of eternal life which God that cannot lie promised before the world began."

If God promised his creatures eternal life before the world began, will they not obtain it? They will for this passage says that he *cannot lie*. But says the objector, he has not promised it to the unbeliever. We would then inquire, what is it that constitutes him an *unbeliever*? Why do you call him an *unbeliever*? Do you say because he disbelieves the truth of God's promise? Then you must, of course, admit the truth of God's promise to him. If so, it must stand, for God cannot lie. You cannot call upon a sinner to *believe*, until you admit the existence of *that very truth*, you wish him to believe, God's promise of eternal life in Christ, is the gospel we are called upon to believe with a sincere heart. If you contend that it is promised to an elect number only, and not to the reprobates, then if they should all be brought to the knowledge of the truth, what would they believe? Ans. The elect would believe the promise of eternal life was made to them, the reprobates would believe right the reverse of the elect, and all would be believers. No, says the objector, the reprobates ought to believe just as the elect do. But in this case, they would believe that they also have the promise of eternal life. This would be believing a lie, because you say that God has not made them that promise? How would you preach to such persons? If you called upon them to believe the truth of the gospel, which is eternal life, you would call upon them to believe a lie. How can you extricate yourself from this difficulty? But inquires the objector, how do you know that God has promised eternal life to all? Ans. Because the scriptures do call all men either *believers*, or *unbelievers*, in view of the promise that God has made. Take away that promise and belief or unbelief respecting it can no longer have an existence— *Believers and unbelievers* would be no more.

But says the objector this is not proof that eternal life is promised to an *unbeliever*. Well I am surprised at this assertion of my opponent! First, I ask, what do you call a believer? Ans. One who believes that God has promised, and given him eternal life in Christ before the world began. Then, of course, an *unbeliever* must be one, to whom God has also promised and given eternal life in Christ before the world, but will not believe it. But says the objector this cannot be. I would then ask whether eternal life was not promised, and given in Christ to the *believer* before he believed it? Certainly. It must have been the truth before he could believe. Well, what was he at that time? An *unbeliever* of course. Then eternal [life] is promised to all, because it is the lack of faith in *that never failing promise* of Jehovah that constitutes an unbeliever. But says the objector—a man "must do so and so," or he cannot be saved. This is not correct; he must *believe*, or he cannot be saved. We are saved by faith in the promise and are permitted to look forward with satisfaction and joy to an immortal existence where we shall be free from sin, sorrow and pain. This faith and hope fill the soul with love to God, and induce us to break off our sins by righteousness. So a salvation by faith can only be enjoyed in this life, and is to end when faith and hope are lost in certainty and in joy. Though only few are saved by faith, yet all shall know the Lord from the greatest to the least, whom to know is life eternal.

SERMON VIII

"Jesus answered and said unto him, Verily, verily, I say unto thee, Except a man be born again, he cannot see the kingdom of God." John iii. 3.

As we have in the last three sermons dwelt particularly on a salvation by *faith*, we will take the liberty to introduce the subject of the new birth next in order, as it will be, more readily, retained by the reader, in this connexion than otherwise. Indeed, it hears a strong resemblance to them so far as the subject of faith is concerned in our present exposition. But whoever is a careful reader of the New Testament, will discover that the subject of faith, and the genuine repentance which that faith produces, is not of trivial moment.

There is no subject of divine revelation, on which more has been said, preached and written than the one, which we are now about to consider. It has been brought forward by men of talents and erudition as an insuperable barrier against Universal Salvation, and their several adherents have taken it for granted, that it can never be explained in harmony with the sentiment, that all men shall eventually obtain eternal life through the Redeemer of men. But these impressions have arisen from the fact, that they have taken their own views and explanations to be scripturally correct, and from these premises, they have drawn conclusions utterly opposed to the final holiness and happiness of God's intelligent creation. They have supposed the new birth to be some mysterious change produced by some mysterious operation of the divine spirit on the mind, and that it is in substance a miracle.

One denomination has contended that if a man once obtained this change, he was safe, could never "finally fall from grace," but would eventually land in the kingdom of immortal glory. Several other denominations admit the new birth to be the same change already noticed, but contend that the subject may fall from grace, and be finally lost. Here then the man, who was, according to their views, *born again*, might still never see the kingdom of God beyond the grave. On this principle the new birth would be no security, that any one would obtain heaven. According to this sentiment, a man might be born again, fall away, and be born again "until seven times," and in the end not see the kingdom of God. Those, who advocate this sentiment, believe that *faith and repentance* prerequisites to the new birth, and also believe in the salvation of infants.

This being so, it will come to pass that half of the world will be saved, inasmuch as about that number die in what may be, justly termed an infant state. But of those, who come to years of accountability, they believe but few will be saved. So the greater proportion of those, who will finally surround the throne of God, will be those, who have never been born again according to their views. It will not, I presume, be contended, that infants who, they believe, are totally depraved, ever exercise *faith*, or experience the *new birth* in this life.

From the above views, I shall take the liberty to dissent, and may probably differ some from the expositions given by others. It is evident that Jesus Christ in his instructions frequently brought forward some natural facts plainly understood by those whom he addressed, in order more clearly to illustrate his subject, and then made his illustrations so nearly resemble that natural fact, that no man could possible misunderstand him, unless he had been led into tradition by blind guides. In the context, he makes allusion to natural birth, of which every man knows the meaning, and says to Nicodemus, "that which is born of the flesh is flesh, and that which is born of the spirit is spirit."

Natural birth pre-supposes the perfect formation of the human body by that secret energy of nature, God only can comprehend. But that formation, itself, is not birth. Birth is that operation, that introduced us into this world. We are now flesh and blood, which cannot inherit the kingdom. What is born of the flesh is flesh. We must now be born again from mortal to immortality, otherwise we could not see the kingdom of God.

Must not man be born of a woman in order to see this world? Can he look upon the beautiful objects of creation, or contemplate these countless wonders of the Almighty before he is born into being? He cannot. All without exception will admit, that it is impossible for any man to enter this natural world, in which we live, without birth. So it is equally impossible to enter the kingdom of God without being born *again* in the strictest sense of the word. A man cannot "be born again" ten, or twenty years, nor even *one day* before he sees the kingdom of God, any more than he could be born twenty days before he came forth out of the womb. As natural birth cannot take place any given time before we enter this world, but is the *circumstance* that introduces us, so a *second birth* cannot take place any given time before we enter the kingdom of God in the next world but is the *very thing*, that shall introduce us into it; and the moment we are born again, we shall see it,—we shall be spirit, and beyond the dominion of death and sin. He that is born of the flesh, *is flesh*, so long as he lives; and he that is born of the spirit *is spirit*. As we now "bear the image of the earthly" through a *natural* birth, "so we shall also bear the image of the heavenly" through a *spiritual* birth. And as no man in this world is a spirit, so no man has in reality passed the new birth. When we were born into this world, we were brought from insensibility to an existence entirely new. So in order to enter the kingdom of God, which is not of this world, we must be born again from the insensibility of death into a new and happy existence beyond the grave.

The question now arises, when does this new birth take place? We reply when this mortal puts on immortality through a resurrection. When we shall be aroused from the sleep of death to a precipient existence in heaven—when we shall awake satisfied with the likeness of God. Paul, in the xv. Chap. 1 Cor. Plainly states that the spiritual body is prepared and put on after death. Birth then must *follow*, not *precede* that spiritual body. It is impossible that birth should take place, till the body is first prepared. Man's natural body is organized in the womb, and then born into this world. He drops to a state of insensibility in death, a reorganization of the spiritual body takes place to the natural eye imperceptible, and its nature indestructible. It is gradually brought forward through a resurrection similar to the grain of wheat to which Paul compares it, is awakened to a conscious existence, and bears the image of the heavenly as it once bore the image of the earthy. The resurrection is therefore every moment progressing, and every man is raised in his own order of time.

But says the reader, if the resurrection be the new birth, then Christ, himself must have been born again, in order to enter the kingdom of God! Certainly. But inquires the reader, where do the scriptures teach that Christ was ever born again? In Colossians chap. i:15. are these words—"Who [Christ] is the image of the invisible God, the *first born* of every creature." This cannot mean that he was the first born into this state of existence; but he was the first one whom human eyes ever saw alive beyond the destruction of death to die no more, and the only one that mortal eye will ever see, for he arose in his natural body, (being the only true witness, appointed of God,) to bring life and immortality to light through the gospel.

But that passage, says the reader, does not satisfy me, that Christ was born again. Then listen once more—verse 18—"who is the beginning, the *first born* from the dead that in all things he might have the pre-eminence." Rev. chap. i. 5. "Jesus Christ the faithful witness, and the *first begotten* from the dead." Here it is plainly stated that he is the "first born from the dead" "the *first begotten* from the dead" These scriptures in connexion with several others, that might be quoted, prove that Christ was born again, and that the resurrection is called birth.

It is evident that man falls to a state of insensibility in death, and remains in sleep while the spiritual body is forming out of those subtle materials, that at death pass into *hades*; and when the reorganization is completed, the new being is born into the kingdom of immortal glory. A drowning man, we know, falls to a state of unconsciousness. Fainting—yes, even a night's sleep proves that the mind is susceptible of falling into insensibility, or suspending its mental operations, and disproves the notion of its entering a future state, only through a resurrection of the dead. This fact is not only substantiated by reason, but it is the doctrine of Revelation. The wise man says, "the dead know not any thing." Paul, in the xv. Chap. 1 Cor. Predicates the truth of our resurrection on the fact that Christ rose from the dead; and on this ground he reasons, that if there be no resurrection, then preaching is vain, faith is also vain, the christians were yet in their sins, and they that were fallen asleep in Christ were perished, and concludes by saying, "let us eat, drink, for tomorrow we die." Suppose a christian should this moment die, and, according to common opinion, enter immediately on an immortal existence. Could we now say—if there be no resurrection, he is fallen asleep in Christ and perished? No, because, instead of being perished, i.e. *Annihilated*, he would remain in infinite happiness and glory, even if there should, never, be any resurrection. So you perceive that Paul did not believe any one could enter eternity only through a resurrection. He believed, they would fall asleep in Christ, and in that sleep remain till in Christ they were made alive. He embraces the whole in the following words—"Since by man came death, by man came also the resurrection of the dead."

When the sentence of death was pronounced upon Adam, which was to pass upon all men, the promise of a Saviour then made, was, it appears, not understood. Their posterity looked forward for a temporal king, and had no idea of an immortal existence beyond the "narrow house." Death the king of terrors, was not yet disarmed of his sting by the resurrection of our triumphant Redeemer. This truth was not yet revealed to men. Here the human family were without hope, and trembling at the darkness—the seven fold darkness of the tomb. No ray of light and joy beamed from that cheerless mansion to ease the aching heart, or dispel that melancholy gloom, which pervaded the parental bosom when gazing for the last time upon the struggles of a dying child.

Here was a world born into existence under the certain sentence of death, and groaning in the bondage of corruption, without any hope of being delivered from it, by an immortal birth, "into the glorious liberty of the children of God." In this period of anxiety and distress, the glad tidings were proclaimed to the shepherds on the plains of Judea, announcing the birth of the Saviour of the world. A new birth, which is not mentioned in the old Testament, was at length proclaimed by a Saviour in the *new*. He died on the cross, and was "the first born from the dead."

He is the head of every man, by the grace of God tasted death for every man, and rose again for their justification. The scriptures declare that "we shall be saved by his life" that he is "the bread of God that cometh down from heaven and giveth life to the world." He is our way, our truth and life, and "because he lives we shall live also." "As in Adam all die, even so in Christ shall all be made alive," or born from the dead. And he that is made alive in Christ is a new creature, old things are passed away—all things are become new.

But says the reader, though the resurrection of Jesus is set forth by a birth from death, yet the resurrection of the human family is never so represented. You mistake. Out of the many passage that might be adduced, we have room, in this discourse, for only one. It shall, however, be satisfactory. In Romans, 8th chapter, Paul says, "Because the creature itself also, shall be delivered from the bondage of corruption into the glorious liberty of the children of God; for we know that the whole creation groaneth and travaileth in pain together until now." [We would remark, that the word *creature, is ktisis* in the Greek, and is the same that is rendered *creation* in the next verse.] In this quotation, you perceive, that Paul represents the whole creation as groaning in travail pains, and declares that the whole creation shall be delivered from the bondage of corruption into the glorious liberty of the sons of God. He compares them to a woman in pain ready for delivery; and that they are delivered from corruption to incorruption at the resurrection is certain. [See 1 Cor. xv:42.]

You now understand what I mean by the new birth. It is to pass from death to life and immortality, in Christ, beyond the grave, where flesh and blood can never enter. For that which is born of the flesh is flesh, and that which is born of the spirit is spirit.

We have now pointed out the new birth, and shown that it bears some resemblance to the natural birth, with which Jesus compared it. And how truly sublime and cheering the thought, that the great family of man, who are all born into existence under the certain sentence of death, are to receive a second birth into an existence entirely new, and the whole of his dying family are to be made the children of Jesus Christ by adoption.

In our next, we shall notice the change we experience in this life, called in scripture the new birth, and explain the term, "kingdom of God."

SERMON IX

"Jesus answered and said unto him, verily, verily, I say unto thee, except a man be born again, he cannot see the kingdom of God." John iii. 3.

In our last, we have shown, that the *spiritual* birth bears some resemblance to a natural birth with which Jesus compared it—and as the *first* introduces us into this world, so the *second* will introduce us into the future and immortal world at the resurrection, where we shall be as the angels of God in heaven, and "be the *children* of God *being the children of the resurrection.*" There we shall be completely free from sin and pain. There the gushing tear of sorrow shall cease to flow, and the brow of disconsolate humanity be ruffled no more.

We will now attend to the present effects that the truth of this birth has upon us here, and notice at the same the phrase, "*kingdom of God.*"

The question now arises; do not some experience the new birth in this life? They do. But in what sense do they experience it? Ans. By *faith*. In this world we pass from death to life: not that we have actually been in the grave and brought to life beyond it; but the believer experiences this by faith. And *this faith* has a most powerful and happifying influence on his affections, and consequently on his life and conduct. All, that God has revealed for the salvation of the world—our justification, our sanctification, our new birth, our heaven, our all—yes, all these important and heavenly changes are summed up, and embraced in our immortal resurrection, will actually take place through death; and while in this world we can embrace them, *only by faith*.

The scriptures declare that "we walk by faith and, not by sight." Paul says, "the life which I now live in the flesh I live by the faith of the Son of God, who loved me, and gave himself for me." Paul knew that he had eternal life given him in Christ, before the world began, and faith in that glorious truth produced a happiness—a divine life in his heart, called the kingdom of God within. Let us notice these several points.

1. First; "Christ rose again for our justification." Our justification then exists in our resurrection state, and will *there* in all its reality take place. But cannot a man be justified *here*? Yes; he can be justified *through faith* in that truth.

2. Second; "By the which will, we are *sanctified* through the offering of the body of Jesus Christ once for all." Our *sanctification* then, by the will of God, will take place through death. But cannot a man be *sanctified* while *here*? Yes; he can be sanctified *through faith in that truth!*

3. Third; Christ was "put to death in the flesh, but quickened by the spirit." So in his resurrection he passed from death to life, and thus revealed the truth that we shall also pass from death to life by the power of God, and be like

him who is the "first fruits." But cannot a man pass from death to life while on earth? Yes; he can pass from death to life *through faith in that truth.* Jesus says—"He that heareth my word and believeth on him that sent me hath everlasting life and shall not come into condemnation but is passed from death unto life."

4. Fourth; our eternal life will be realized beyond death. "The things that are not seen are spiritual and eternal." But can we not enjoy it *here*? Yes; "He that believeth on the Son *hath* everlasting life;"— that is, he enjoys it faith.

5. Fifth; Christ was the "first born from the dead." So we also shall pass the reality of the new birth by faith. But can we not enjoy it here? John says—"For whatsoever is born of God overcometh the world, and this is the victory that overcometh world *even our faith.*"

Thus it is evident that a man may in this life be *justified, sanctified*, pass from *death to life, may enjoy eternal life*, and be *born again* through faith in *these several correspondent facts.* His faith, however, can make them no more *certain*; because they *must exist*, and be solemn and unalterable facts before he can be called upon to believe them. The truth of the above *five facts*, we perceive, are embraced in our resurrection. If we are not, in our resurrection, to be *justified, sanctified, born again*, and obtain eternal life, then we cannot be *justified, sanctified or born again here* through faith in those truths;—because there would be no such truths in existence for us to exercise faith in. If the objector will not allow these facts unalterably to exist *previous* to believing, what then will he call upon us to believe? Will he call upon us to believe that we have an eternal life in Christ when no such fact exists, and contend that our believing this lie will create the fact? This would be the most ridiculous absurdity.

But the truth exists, and the believer by faith enjoys it before hand. He enjoys it by anticipation, not in *reality*. It can be brought to his understanding or experience no other way, only through the gospel medium of faith. I challenge the objector to show me between the lids of the new Testament, any regeneration, new birth, justification, or sanctification, that has already taken place in any other sense than through faith. All these things in their *reality* are to take place in our resurrection, when we shall be like the angels of God and by faith we bring them present to our minds and enjoy them *here*. Dr. Watts says—"Faith brings distant prospects home, Of things a thousand years ago, Or thousand years to come." Paul, therefore, exhorts us to forget the things that are behind, and reach forward to those that are before—to press to the mark &c. because the reality—the object of our faith lies before us. But persons, who do not understand the operations of faith on the mind in view of its correspondent truth, and who honestly believe that the new birth has in reality already taken place with them, are always looking back to the time they were born again, and telling over their "old experiences" Now this is right in them, if they have passed through the *reality*; for every man ought to look to the substance in which he exercises faith and hope. But certainly the scriptures exhort us to look forward, and anchor our faith and hope within the vail, where our forerunner hath for us entered. It is therefore certain that the reality exists there, and is yet to come. Such persons then, in looking back to their experience, are mistaking the birth produced by faith for the real birth itself. This is just as unreasonable as it would be to suppose that the foretaste, we sometimes enjoy of immortal life, was that life itself. It is true we at times enjoy a heaven on earth. But as it respects the kingdom of immortal glory, "eye hath not seen, ear heard, neither hath it entered into the heart of man to conceive the glory that shall be revealed in us." The reality is therefore yet to come, and by faith we receive only an antepast of its joys.

From the above observation we infer that, the resurrection is the only gospel faith and hope of a future, happy conscious state of being. When our minds are enlightened to see the mighty changes, that we mortals are represented, in the scriptures of truth, as destined to experience by being raised in a holy and deathless constitution, we are then led to consider the resurrection of embracing all those realities that we are called upon by Jesus Christ and his apostles to embrace by faith and enjoy in this life. So great and sublime is the gift of God, and so far surpassing thought does it magnify the perfections of the divine character, and in so amiable a light does it manifest his love to the children of men, that a living faith in its reality cannot but obtain a salutary influence on our life and conversation. So much stress did the apostles lay upon its importance, that they went every where preaching the resurrection of the dead, as the gospel of Christ.

There is one point we will here notice. All denominations acknowledge that for any man *by faith* to pass from death to life is a change for the better. If so, then the *reality*, namely to pass from the sleep of death to an immortal existence, must be a change for the better. Because it is by believing that future reality we are said to have passed from death to life here. The conclusion is unavoidable that the *reality* must correspond with its antepast *by faith*. To understand this let us reverse it. Suppose it should be an established law in the nature and constitution of things that all mankind should pass from death to immortal misery in the future world. Let this be revealed and proclaimed as an unchanging truth. As many as believed it would of course pass from death to immortal misery in *faith*, which would lead them to curse the being who made them, and destined them to this unhappy end. It would be a change for the worse.

Our subject is now so far plain (according to our views) that the phrase "*kingdom of God*" will be readily understood. Though it has, by different writers, been made to bear many different significations, yet we shall take the liberty to contend that it simply means as follows—1. First an immortal existence beyond the grave brought to light by the resurrection of Christ;—and 2. Second a belief in *that reality* is the kingdom of God we here enter and enjoy *by faith*. Into this kingdom, infants, idiots and heathen and unbelievers do not enter, because faith is the only condition. This is the kingdom of heaven that men, blind leaders of the blind, shut up. They neither enter themselves, nor suffer those that would enter to go in. They keep the evidence of the reality out of sight so that men cannot look beyond the vail to its brighter glories and enjoy its peaceful reign in their hearts by faith. When faith is lost in certainty, *then* this kingdom will be delivered up, and to know shall be life eternal. This definition we believe will hold good, and apply to any passage in the New Testament where it may occur. Though some contend that it very seldom has reference to an immortal existence, yet we strenuously contend that there is no propriety in the phrase only in connexion with such an existence. We cannot enter or be born into the kingdom of God by faith, unless we admit the reality in the first place to have an existence, any more than we could, by faith, enjoy eternal life unless there is such a reality as eternal life beyond the grave. The above, the reader will please to fix in his mind.

We now perceive that man drops into the sleep of death, and that the resurrection, or new birth is his only hope of a future happy state of existence, and is the only change that can free him from imperfection, and sin, and make him a new creature in a new and immortal existence beyond the grave.

We will here introduce an example to make our argument so far plain. Suppose you were now in ignorance respecting the doctrine of life and immortality through a resurrection. You know you must die, and sincerely think that death will terminate your existence forever. You see your children one after another laid upon their dying bed, and with distraction shake the farewell hand of eternal separation, and with the most solemn melancholy and wo, look forward to the period when you must follow them down to the chambers of eternal silence, and cease to be.

In this moment of dread solemnity and gloom, suppose some kind angel should appear at the bed-side of your expiring child, and kindly inquire, why are you troubled? You answer, because my children have fallen!—the last of my infant train lies panting for breath, and the dreadful hour has come when all those silken affections, that build our hearts love, must be rent assunder, and in the awful bosom of death, be extinguished forever!—Suppose your guardian angel smiling over the ruins of death, should point you far beyond these changing scenes, and with rapture exclaim, you shall meet this darling child again and commingle with your little fallen flock in glory! You and they and all mankind shall be born from the dead into the kingdom of God, and be new creatures free from sin and pain, and "be the children of God being the children of the resurrection." Jesus your Lord "was the first born from the dead," and you shall pass from death to life and live forever.

Now suppose you positively believed his words; could you not say in the scripture form of the expression that through faith you was already "passed from death to life?"—that you was born of faith, and by faith was in the kingdom of God? You certainly could, and it would in every sense of the word be true. Through faith, you would be justified, through faith sanctified; through faith you would enjoy eternal life—in fine, through faith you would be saved. This faith would give love unmeasured to your Creator, and fill your soul with joy unspeakable and full of glory. "Faith works by love, purifies the heart and overcomes the world."

Reader, do you not love the Lord for his wonderful goodness to his children? What glorious hopes are here! "and he that hath this hope in him purifieth himself even as he is pure"—you now see why the gospel rings with the word *faith* from one end to the other.

The world previous to the coming of Jesus Christ had no knowledge of immortality through a resurrection, into the kingdom of God. The phrase "*born again*" is not mentioned in the Old Testament, and of course means something more than a *conversion*. This subject will be continued in our next.

SERMON X

"Jesus answered and said unto him, verily, verily, I say unto thee, except a man be born again, he cannot see the kingdom of God." John iii. 3.

The literal rendering of this passage seems to be—"*except a man be born above.*" The word *above* being substituted for *again* more forcibly demonstrates the correctness of my views in the two former discourses.

Many charge the Universalists with denying the necessity of a new birth, or regeneration. But take from me my faith and hope in that glorious truth, and I must at that moment resign the salvation of every human being. Convince me that not another child will be born into this world, and you will at once convince me that this world will shortly be destitute of a solitary inhabitant. Convince me that a man will not be born again, and you will not only convince me that no one will ever enter the kingdom of God, but that the many worlds, that have already passed from the stage of mortal being, and those that shall hereafter follow, will alike be consigned to eternal silence! Endless misery is out of the question. That could have had no existence even had there been no resurrection in *Him* who is the life of the world; but death would have terminated the existence of all. Such a punishment is not threatened in all the writings of Moses and the prophets. And we cannot reasonably suppose, if such were a principal truth in revelation, that God would suffer four thousand years to elapse without warning his creatures of such an awful doom. Upon our first parents, for transgressing the law, he pronounced all the miseries of life, and uttered the closing sentence, "Dust thou art and unto dust shalt thou return." Here the doctrine of endless misery (if that be the sentence of the violated law) ought to have been clearly stated to the "covenant head" of our race, so that the same sentence might pass upon all that have sinned, unless they complied with the conditions set before them.

But we leave this point, and will notice the 5th verse which may, perhaps, be considered as an objection to my views, and urged as proof that the new birth is wholly confined to this life. "Except a man be born of *water*, and of the spirit," &c. What is here meant by "*water*"? Ans. Baptism by immersion. This, instead of being an objection to my views, will strengthen them. Baptism in water is nothing more than a *figure* of our death and resurrection, by *which* we manifest our *faith* in the resurrection of the dead, by which *faith* our hearts are baptized into the spirit and truth of the gospel of Christ.

Paul says, I Cor. xv:29 "Else what shall they do, which are baptized for the dead, if the dead rise not at all? Why are they then baptized for the dead?" Baptism being only a *figure* of our death and resurrection, is perhaps, in a gospel sense, of but little consequence to christians in the present day.

Christ went to John and was baptized of him in Jordan. His being put under water signified his death, when the condemning power of the law under the first dispensation should lose its force—and his being raised out of the water signified his resurrection from the cold Jordan of death to immortal life in the kingdom of God, where the victory shall be sung over *death and sin*; and over the *law* which "is the strength of sin." Having passed in figure through his own death and resurrection, and having manifested to man that he was baptized by the Holy Spirit into the faith and "powers of the world to come," he perfectly lived up to his obligation, by never committing one sin. He went through life free from transgression as though he were already in eternity. When his crucifixion hour approached, he said, [Luke xii:50] "I have a baptism to be baptized with, and how am I straitened" [Greek—pained] "till it be accomplished." Here he had reference to his being buried in death, (which was to be attended with extreme sufferings) and rising again from it, which would be the *reality* of which his baptism in Jordan was but a *figure*.

To be put under water signifies our *death*, and to be raised out again signifies our *resurrection*. A person, who is baptized, ought therefore, to endeavor, as much as in him lies, to live as though he were already in his resurrection state. Enjoying in faith the baptism of the "Holy Spirit and of fire," he ought to consider himself as dead to the world and alive to God walking in newness of life.

Let us introduce Rom. vi:3, 4. "Know ye not that so many of us as were baptized into Jesus Christ, were baptized into *his death*? Therefore we are buried with him by baptism into death; that like as Christ was raised up from the dead by the glory of the Father, even so we also should walk in newness of life." Here we perceive they were baptized into his death, and were rejoicing in hope of the *resurrection*, having their hearts purified faith in the reality, Acts xxii. 16 And now why tarriest thou? Arise, and be baptized, and wash away thy sins, &c. Now, it is not only a scripture doctrine, but all denominations acknowledge, that baptism in water is an *emblem* of the washing away of our sins. We then ask—are our sins to be wished in a stream of water? No. Where then? The objector says, our sins are taken away *in this life* by the baptism of the "Holy Spirit and with fire." This cannot be; because Paul told the believers that if there were no resurrection, their faith was vain, and they were *yet in their sins*. [See I. Cor. xv. 17.] This proves that believers receive the forgiveness of their sins in this life *by faith only*, not in *reality*.

The question returns, are our sins washed away in a stream of water? No. Where then? Ans. Through death and the resurrection, for that is the real baptism. And it is certain that the *reality* must embrace all that the *figure* in water teaches. We then solemnly ask the reader,—if baptism in water is a *figure* of our death and resurrection, and if *that water baptism* signifies the washing away of our sins, will not then our sins be washed away through death and the resurrection? Yes; otherwise the figure in water has no meaning.

Thus we perceive that being born of the water is no objection to our views of the new birth, but affords them an unshaken support. If any one contend that the sins of our race are not to be taken away through death, we would then ask, where will the christian's sins be washed away? The scriptures declare that there is not a just man upon earth that doeth good and sinneth not,—and if there is no change through death then there will not be a just man beyond the grave that doeth good and sinneth not. But the baptism "with the Holy Spirit and with fire" in all its solemn and interesting reality will take place in death and the resurrection, and to exercise a living faith in that truth, so as to influence our life and conduct according to the spirit of the gospel, is what the scriptures term being baptized with the spirit and with fire in this life. But this present enjoyment is not the *reality*, but an antepast of *that reality*; because "we walk by faith and not by sight." It is immaterial whether the scripture speaks of *pardon, of justification; of sanctification, of redemption, of regeneration, or baptism* "with the Holy Spirit and with fire," it simply means that those facts in the divine counsels unchangeably exist, and will burst upon the whole groaning creation in the resurrection world, while the believer only enjoys them in this state of being through faith, which baptizes him into the spirit of Christ. But if there be no resurrection, and nought is presented to our anticipation but the dreary prospect of a beamless eternity, then "preaching is vain," "faith is also vain," "christians are yet in their sins," "and they that are fallen asleep in Christ are perished."

The taking away the sin of the world by the Lamb of God, who is the resurrection and the life, is through death. Through death, to our faith and hope, he has destroyed "him who hath the power of death, that is the devil." The washing away of all sin, by the power of God, is through death and the resurrection. *Then* and not till then shall the song of triumph be sung by redeemed millions—"O death! Where is thy sting? O grave! Where is thy victory? The sting of death is sin, and the strength of sin is the law", &c.

All the figures of baptism point to *death*—all the sacrifices for sin, slain under the law for 4000 years, point to death, declaring that without the shedding of blood there is no remission. There the reality lies. There we are called upon to anchor our faith and hope even within the veil. And it must be a *certain truth* that our sins are to be washed away through the Jordan of death, before we can be called upon to believe it. It must be a *certain reality* that sin is there to be purged away, before we could, with any propriety, use baptism in water as a shadow of it; because the *shadow* cannot create the *substance*.

We have now shown that as man is naturally born into this world, so he shall be spiritually born into the kingdom of God. We have shown by comparison that except a man be born of a woman, he cannot see this world; and as this does not mean that he must be born twenty days before he comes forth from the womb, as a preparation for entering this world, so the expression, "except a man be born again he cannot see the kingdom of God," does not mean that he must be born twenty days before death as a preparation for entering a future existence. The new birth, no more means a *reality* that is to transpire *here*, than natural birth means some change we underwent prior to our being brought forth into life.

I believe in all the reformation or new birth here that others do, and believe in much more to come. That change *here*, which they call the new birth, I call the new birth in faith, or being born of faith, while the solemn reality is yet to transpire, and that is to be born from the dead in Christ our head. These facts we will now make plain to every reader by the following example, so that our views on this subject may not be misrepresented.

Suppose that before we were born, we had been able to conceive ideas. And suppose it had been spoken to us by the Son of God—except you are born of the flesh, you cannot see the natural world, which is most beautiful to to behold, having sun, moon, and stars, and songsters, fields and groves. It has never entered your heart to conceive the glory to be revealed in you. Now suppose some of us had believed this revelation, we would that moment, have been born of faith, and rejoiced in hope of the glory to be revealed in us; and by faith have looked forward to the reality. This, however, would not have made our birth any more certain, because it must have been an absolute truth before we could have, with any propriety, believed it. Suppose, further, that some of us had rejected it; would this circumstance have prevented our being born? Certainly not. All of us, who believed, would have been born of faith, having an earnest of the reality, and the unbelievers would have come short of that enjoyment by faith; but their unbelief could in no sense make the truth of none effect. The moment we were born, belief and unbelief would be lost in certainty.

Now suppose that some of had said—the Son of God has declared "except we are born of the flesh, we cannot see the natural world." This must mean some great change we are to experience in the womb—we must be born some number of days before we enter the natural world, as a preparation, otherwise we can never see it.

We now ask the reader, whether it would not be folly to give to the word *birth* such an explanation? The Conclusion is unavoidable. We then ask, whether it does not involve the same folly to contend, in view of our text, ("except a man be born again, he cannot enter into the kingdom of God") that it means, he must be born again in this world, as a preparation for another? It certainly does.

We once more repeat it—that as natural birth was the *very thing* that introduced us all into this world of imperfection, sorrow and pain; so the spiritual birth will be the *very thing*, that shall introduce us all into another, where, imperfection, sorrow and pain shall be no more.

The poor heathen, and infants, and all, will therefore be born again into the kingdom of God, and "be equal unto the angels, die no more, and be the children of God, *being the children of the resurrection*." The only advantage we enjoy above them is, that we have heard the good news, believed it, are "born again, not of corruptible seed, but of incorruptible, by the word of God which liveth and abideth forever," and "have entered into rest." We are rejoicing in hope of the glory of God to be revealed in us, while they are groping in darkness, inasmuch, as they cannot believe in him of whom they have not heard.

In our next, we shall close this subject by urging the importance of the new birth through faith in the truth.

SERMON XI

"Jesus answered and said unto him, verily, verily, I say unto thee, except a man be born again, he cannot see the kingdom of God." John iii. 3.

In our last three discourses we have endeavoured to lay our views of the new birth thus far plainly before the reader, and wish him to bear in mind that the three sermons, preceding those on the new birth, are also to be read, and carefully kept in view, so that, from the whole connexion, the gospel doctrine of salvation by *faith* may be made clear to his understanding. We dwelt so long, and laid so much stress upon *faith*, because it is the *first* christian grace, we are exhorted to put on, and is the *first* assent of the mind to the great and interesting *truth* revealed in the gospel of Jesus Christ, which is *life and immortality* for the human family.

We have shown that the new birth has a higher signification than simply to be converted from the evil of our doings, as was required under the first dispensation. The new birth, so far as it concerns the present existence, embraces not only *conversion*, but the whole spiritual life of the christian's soul, denominated the kingdom of heaven within. This mental felicity—this "weight of glory," cannot be enjoyed, but by the exercise of a living faith in Christ. Such a faith begets a sincere obedience in our life and conversation. It is a faith "that works by love, purifies the heart and overcomes the world." The great apostle to the Gentiles exclaims—"the life that I now live in the flesh, I live by the *faith* of Son of God, who loved me and gave himself for me." We therefore "walk by *faith*, not by *sight*."

We have shown that Christ was the *"first born* from the dead" to show light to the people and to the Gentiles, and that the whole creation is groaning in travail-pains, and that it shall be delivered from the bondage of corruption into the glorious liberty of the children of God, and that we shall then be as the angels of God in heaven. We have shown that all mankind—infants, idiots and heathen, shall be brought to realize this birth, and that the believer, only, can only enjoy it in this state of existence through *faith* in the truth, and that this *faith* has a most powerful influence on his life and conversation, "being born of incorruptible seed by the word of God that liveth and abideth forever." We have shown that neither this birth, nor any of the spiritual changes, can be experienced in this life only through *faith* in their correspondent truths, even as they are revealed to us in the gospel of Christ. We have shown that by the phrase, "kingdom of heaven" we were to understand, *first*, a holy, happy and immortal existence "beyond the grave, incorruptible, undefiled and that fadeth not away, reserved for us in heaven," and which, with all its perfections and joys, was revealed to us by Jesus Christ; and *second*, a sincere and living *faith* in this interesting *reality*, produced that divine enjoyment, called "the kingdom of heaven within us," the kingdom of heaven among men, &c. This kingdom the Pharisees "shut up"—they "neither entered it themselves, nor suffered those that were entering to go in." That is—they prevented the people from *believing* those interesting *realities*—those sublime doctrines of a future world that their Messiah had brought to light through the gospel for the present happiness of men.

We have shown that water baptism is but a *figure, a shadow* of our death and resurrection, or of the washing of regeneration and renewing of the Holy Spirit, and that this figure is of but little consequence to us in this present day. In fine we have shown that if there were no future existence—if nought were held up to man but the dreary prospect of a beamless eternity, he could not be justified, sanctified, born again, pass from death to life or enter the kingdom of God through faith, because in such case the *objects* of his *faith and hope* would be annihilated, his faith would be vain, he would be yet in his sins. In this view of our subject, we perceive that Christ is but "the author and finisher of our faith," having been ordained of God "to bring life and immortality to light," to set us an example for our imitation and happiness here below—and to die and rise in attestation of the truth involved in his mission. Consequently his kingdom will be delivered up when *faith and hope* shall be lost in certainty and joy.

It now remains that we urge the importance of the *new birth* through faith in the truth. And here we shall probably meet with one objection from the reader, viz. As we argued in sermons, No. 5, 6, and 7, that faith was the first exercise of the creature, and that no one could *believe or disbelieve* what he pleased, the reader may then ask, what necessity is there of urging the importance of the new birth through faith in the truth, in as much as faith cannot be exercised at the *pleasure* or simply at the *will* of man? And here we would remark— that the guilt of unbelief does not consist in rejecting a fact after patient investigation, by collecting all the evidences in our reach, but it consists in rejecting a fact without examination of its truth. For instance; let the gospel be preached to a heathen, who rejects it without attempting to acquaint himself with the evidences upon which its truth is based. He is condemned for not believing, because he neglects the only means by which he might be convinced of the truth. He declines searching for evidence. Of the truth of this remark we have a striking instance in the scriptures. Paul preached at Thessalonica, but they heeded not his words. He preached also at Berea, and the inspired penman says, "These were more noble than those in Thessalonica, in that they received the word with all readiness of mind, and searched the scriptures daily whether these things were so." It is our duty to search the scriptures prayerfully and "labor to enter into that rest that remains to the people of God, lest any of us through unbelief should seem to come short of it." It is our duty to search for evidence of the fact, at least on all subjects relating to our present happiness, and particularly those that appertain to the future world. They are too momentous to be treated with indifference.

There is nothing more important than that we should exercise a living *faith* in a future and happy existence beyond the grave. This alone can afford the mind "joy unspeakable and full of glory." There is in every human bosom an unceasing uneasiness, an aching void that nothing on earth can satisfy or fill. Old and young, ignorant and learned, heathen and christian feel the same dissatisfaction with the objects of momentary duration. The heathen, in the midst of all his self-denials and self-tortures to appease his gods, and in the conscientious discharge of all his devotional duties, is still a dissatisfied and miserable being. God has so constituted the human mind that it cannot repose in error, however sincere may be the faith it exercises. There is still a growing vacuum within that nothing but the powers of truth can fill. Philosophy has endeavoured to search out that system of moral duties, in the rigid performance of which, that happiness, peace and joy might be found, for which all mortal beings pant with the same aspirations of strong desire, but has sought in vain. From the earliest ages, one system after another has been invented, and in succession abandoned, but all have come short of discovering any thing solid on which to rest their hopes of earthly felicity.

Jesus Christ, the author and finisher of our faith, has alone accomplished what all the penetration of Pythagoras and all the moral lessons of Seneca and Socrates failed to discover. With a bold, firm and untrembling hand he has drawn aside the curtains of the tomb, and pointed the human family to a second birth from the dark womb of death into mansions of incorruptible felicity in the kingdom of God, where they shall die no more, and where all the inquietudes, appertaining to this fleeing existence, shall be unknown. This future state of being, he has not only revealed, but has demonstrated its certainty by those incontestable evidences, which can never be shaken by all the powers of infidelity combined. He has burst the icy bands of death and risen triumphant beyond its solemn shade, and begot in us those lively hopes, those fond desires, that ease the aching heart—that communicate unbroken peace amidst the various ills of life, and afford it divine consolation and joy in the trying moment of death. In those interesting truths the believer confides, and in every condition in life is enabled to rejoice in the hope that when "this earthly tabernacle is dissolved, he has a building of God, a house not made with hands eternal in the heavens." In this faith, man's countless wants are satisfied, inasmuch as God has secured his dearest interest. In this faith the believer is entered into rest, is born of God, and is translated into his kingdom. He *knows* that by faith he has passed from death unto life, for his soul is filled with love to God and man. This love, this divine enjoyment, is the natural effect of *faith*, inasmuch as it works by love, purifies the heart and overcomes, the world. He is not only at rest respecting himself, but at rest respecting his children and dear friends, whom he may be called to follow to the land of silence and the shadow of death. He stands at their dying bed and whispers to them consolation, in the joyful assurance, that he shall meet them again beyond the dominion of death and pain in the regions of glory. His bosom is the mansion of those pure and holy affections and of those sublime hopes, that none can know but those who are thus born into the kingdom of God.

Reader, you must die. How important then that you should faithfully and prayerfully examine the scriptures so that tormenting fears, distraction and despair may not in that solemn moment rend the peace of your bosom to atoms. A sweet peace and composure of soul in that trying hour, are of incalculable worth. It is enough to struggle with physical pain without the addition of mental woes, which present neglect, and your ignorance of the truth and consolations of the gospel of Christ, are sure to bring upon you. Perhaps you are a father, and may be called to stand at the death-bed of a beloved child. That child may call upon you as a parent to administer consolation to its departing spirit. He clings to life, or ardently desires to live forever in the mansions of rest beyond the grave. But what consolation can you impart, if you are yourself ignorant of the doctrines of the gospel of Christ? The heart-rending prospect of endless wo, or the gloomy horrors of annihilation, could afford no consolation to that mind, which has the principles of glory deeply rooted in its nature and which nothing but the continuance of existence can rationally satisfy. As you value unbroken peace in the hour of dissolution, and as you value the happiness of these dear pledges heaven has lent you, study for the evidence of christian truth, search the scriptures, and labor to enter into that rest that remains here to the believing people of God, who are born again and *specially* saved through *faith* in the truth.

This labor is not only important in view of the solemn hour of death, but important in view of the life you here live in the flesh. Happiness is the ultimate pursuit of all mortal beings. They vainly imagine that it can be found in riches, honors and titles—yes, even imagine that it can be found in the hard ways of the transgressor. Though sensible that worlds before them have failed, and gone down to the grave with the pangs of disappointed hope, yet man is so strangely inconsistent as still to believe, that these earthly pursuits contain some hidden charm which he flatters himself he shall find even though all before him have failed. Here is the delusion, kind reader, of which you are cautioned to beware. There is no happiness but in the path where the hand of mercy has sown it—no happiness but in the objects where God has placed it. It is no where to be found but in the enjoyment of the religion of Christ. This will sweeten every earthly pursuit, make every burden light, afford solid enjoyment in life and divine consolation in the hour of death. Flatter not yourself that there is any happiness beneath the sun aside from this. "There is no peace saith my God to the wicked," and, he who says there is, contradicts Jehovah, and is yet "in the gall of bitterness and in the bond of iniquity." A speculative faith is of but little consequence, so long as it does not influence our life and conversation for the better. We must believe to the saving of the soul from the evil of the world. "Then shall thy light break forth as the morning, and thy righteousness shall go before thee, and the glory of the Lord shall be thy reward."

SERMON XII

"A good name is rather to be chosen than great riches, and loving favor rather than silver and gold." Prov. xxii:1.

A good name involves all that can render man exalted and amiable, or life desirable. The good opinion of mankind has, in all ages, been considered as a blessing of the first magnitude, and has, in various ways, been sought for by all. There is no man so dishonest, but what labors to impress upon others the conviction of his honesty; no man so deceptive, but what wishes to be considered sincere; nor cowardly, but desires to be reputed brave; and no man is so abandonedly vicious, but what desires to be considered virtuous by his fellow creatures. All choose a good name in preference to a bad one. This being a fact the appearance of virtue is kept up where the reality is wanting, and the shadow is often mistaken for the substance.

There are many, that are, at heart, insincere and false, who pass in society generally for persons of sincerity, candor and virtue, while their real principles are known only in their own families and among their confidential friends. They desire a good name and outwardly maintain it, while they in reality but little deserve it. In order to know what a man really is, we must be acquainted, not only with his public, but his private character. In his own family, every man appears what he really is. There the heart, word and action art in unison. They embrace each other. In public, they too often separate; and the word, or action, speaks what its divorced companion, the heart does not feel.

Such not only literally choose, but often bear a good name. But this is not the choice suggested by the text. All men, even the most vicious, in some sense or other, choose a good name. But the passage under consideration has a higher, a nobler aim, than a mere choice unconnected with virtuous principle and action. It has a higher aim, than to encourage men to be rotten at heart, and by an outward, hypocritical maneuver, maintain a good name among their fellow creatures. By the text, we are to understand, that a man should early cultivate, in his heart, a virtuous principle, as the pure source from which all those outward actions spring that justly merit the esteem of mankind, force approbation even from the vicious, and thus entitle him to that good name which is far above all price. This will not only afford its possessor unbroken peace arising from the inward consolations and joys of virtuous sincerity, but it will also open to him another rich fountain of felicity, arising from the consideration, that he enjoys the confidence and esteem of the great and the good, with whom he is conversant in life, of his intimate friends, of his companion and children, and above all the smiles of kind heaven and the approbation of his God. His life is calm; his sleep is sweet and associated with golden dreams. No fearful spectres haunt his brain, but the kind angel of mercy is ever at his side. He looks forward to death undismayed, yes, with satisfaction and composure looks beyond that dark scene, to brighter worlds and more substantial joys. He feels the assurance, that even when he shall be here no more, his name shall live in the hearts of those he left behind, be embalmed in the memory of the just, and that it is beyond the power of rolling ages to sully it. This is what we understand by choosing a good name as stated in our text.

Of the truth of this, there can arise no misapprehension when we compare it with the subsequent phrase with which it is contrasted—"a good name is rather to be chosen than great riches, and loving favor than silver and gold." By the choosing of riches, we are to understand, not only a desire to obtain them, but that this desire shall be sufficiently strong to prompt us to use all the honorable and efficient means in our power to accumulate them. The wise man did not mean that every man had the offer of a fortune, and could possess himself of it by simply making choice of it independent of means. No— his choice must be manifested by industry and economy. The means must be used to secure the end. Just so in acquiring a good name. The person desirous of obtaining it, must pursue that upright and virtuous course of conduct, which alone could insure it. And just as well might a man expect riches by being indolent and extravagant, as to expect a good name by indulging in every species of vice. We are therefore to understand our text thus—A good name, through pursuing a virtuous course of conduct, is rather to be chosen than great riches, through the plans and means by which they are obtained.

Man is a being of many wants, and to supply them he is too much inclined to forsake the path of virtue and resort to dishonorable means to obtain wealth.

In view of this master-passion for earthly splendor and greatness, Solomon uttered the words of our text to recall the giddy mind from its chase of shadows, sad turn it to the only source of unmingled felicity in the pursuit of virtue. This would afford the mind those rational delights that wealth, with all its dazzling splendors, cannot impart. It does not possess the charm to convey unbroken peace to the heart.

But there is a strong inducement to engage in a virtuous course, because it is the surest road to wealth and honor. The thief and robber were never rich, nor nor could they be happy if they were. An excellent writer, observes—the importance of a good character in the commerce of life, seems to be universally acknowledged. To those who are to make their own way either to wealth or honors, a good character is as necessary as address and ability. Though human nature is often degenerate, and corrupts itself by many inventions, yet it usually retains to the last an esteem for excellence. But even if we arrive at such an extreme degree of depravity as to have lost our native reverence for virtue, yet a regard to our own interest and safety will lead us to apply for aid, in all important transactions, to men whose integrity is unimpeached. When we choose an assistant or a partner, our first inquiry is concerning his character. When we have occasion for a counsellor, an attorney, or a physician, whatever we may be ourselves, we always choose to trust our property and lives to men of the best character. When we fix on the tradesman, who is to supply us with necessaries, we are we are influenced by fair reputation and honorable dealing. Young men, therefore, whose characters are yet unfixed, and who consequently may render them just such as they wish, ought to pay great attention to the first steps they take on entrance into life. They are usually careless and inattentive to this object. They pursue their own plans with ardor, and neglect the opinions which others entertain of them. By some thoughtless action or expression, they suffer a mark to be impressed upon them, which no subsequent merit can entirely erase. Every man will find some persons who, though they are not professed enemies, yet view him with an eye of envy, and who would gladly revive any tale to which truth has given the slightest foundation.

Though a good name is rather to be chosen than great riches, and is the surest road to wealth, yet there are thousands, who pay but little attention to possess themselves of so valuable a treasure. They turn a deaf ear to that hallowed voice, which pleads with them in behalf of their dearest interest, and take the downward road to dissipation and vice, and, by their wretched example, lead other thousands to the dark abodes of sorrow, grief and pain. Enchanted by the siren voice of false and fleeting pleasure, they hurry to the tremendous precipice, where reputation and fortune lie in broken ruins. There they drag out a wretched existence in disappointed hope, satiety and disgust. They pay their devotions at the shrine of ignominy, where the dark and stagnant waters of guilt and condemnation roll. There the sweet voice of heaven-born peace was never heard, and the beauteous feet of religion never trod. There dwells the family of pain—there is the hell we are cautioned to avoid. This is not an illusion of fancy—it is no reverie of the brain, but a reality too visible in the pathway of human life.

Thousands, in this condition, are hurrying to a premature grave, and go down to that dark abode covered with infamy, having robbed themselves of all the substantial joys, that a virtuous conduct, and a good unsullied name are calculated to awaken in the heart. Dissipation darkens the brightest prospects of life. It rolls its floods of misery indiscriminately over the dearest earthly hopes of companions, children and friends, and paralyzes every pulse of joy that beats in the human bosom. Many a child has been spurned from the presence of its brutal father, and been beaten for asking bread to satisfy its hunger. Intemperance stupefies man to the moral impressions of the gospel, and hardens the heart with the touch of its benumbing powers. It is the giant of human wo that slays his thousands and prostrates the happiness of man. This champion of human war draws his sword of vengeance against the balmy repose of public and private life, and his fatal touch withers the brightest flowers of domestic hope and joy, and mingles the poisonous bowl with the bitter drugs of misery. His government is absolute monarchy, and his subjects the most contemptible slaves. When he lays upon them his cursed hand, they reel to the ground. When he strikes the stunning blow, they drop insensibly to the earth. The oppressions and scourges of the most wretched slave are enviable in comparison with those severe wounds inflicted by this merciless tyrant, this infernal scourge of the human race. Intemperance is a monster that may well be personified. He frolicks through the blood, preys upon the vitals, ploughs up the brain, dethrones reason and laughs at the feeble resistance of the best constitution, and finally bears down all opposition before him. Like the devouring flame, he presses on with irresistible force, urging his deadly siege, till he consumes all that is fair and lovely in the eye of virtue. His present gifts are poverty misery and distress, and his capital prize, a premature grave.

This champion is ravaging our beloved country, and seducing her sons of freedom to the disgraceful ranks of slavery and oppression. Intemperance is that tyrant that has under his control many formidable evils that infest the world. His boasted labor is to hurry on thousands of victims to the commission of crime, and bring down upon them the many misfortunes that attend man in this mutable world. Intemperance involves public broils, tumults and disturbances, and domestic discord, misery and strife.

We trust the number among our readers is small, who are so regardless of a good name as to have abandoned themselves to the intoxicating bowl, or who have sundered all the ties of moral obligation, determined to tread the downward path of vice to a disgraceful tomb. We hope they have a higher regard to the invaluable worth of a good name; and we pray that they may venerate its price far above the momentary glitter of silver and gold. That shall live, when wealth shall have lost its lustre, and flourish immortal, when gold shall have corroded to dust.

Blasphemy is another unreasonable vice against which the public speaker or writer should raise his voice. And let no one flatter himself because we believe in the universal and unbounded goodness of God, that a man may go on as he please. So long as a Being of infinite wisdom is enthroned in the heavens and governs the universe, so long he can never fail to measure out to every offence its adequate punishment, and has all the means at his disposal to bring it unavoidably upon the head of every transgressor. He, who flatters himself that he can sin with impunity, is ignorant of the government of his God, and has never reflected upon human life in all its varied lights and shades. Do you profess to be a Universalist, and yet treat with irreverence the name of HIM who made you, and whom you acknowledge to be a faithful Creator—an indulgent Father? Your professions are nothing. "He that hath this hope in him purifieth himself even as he is pure." That very breath by which he inflates the lungs, can you breathe it back in blasphemies against his holy name, which angels never pronounce but with veneration and awe? Choose, O choose a good name, which can only be obtained by choosing a virtuous course of conduct. However lightly you may treat your own station in life, or however much you may disregard the dignity of your nature, yet remember the station you hold, however obscure, is stamped with responsibility. You are surrounded by a generation of youth, among whom are your own children, ready to imitate your example. Do you wish them well! Then guard your heart and life by setting a reasonable value on a good name, and remember you cannot move without touching some string that may vibrate long after your head rests on its cold pillow of earth.

SERMON XIII

"A good name is rather to be chosen than great riches, and loving favor rather than silver and gold." Prov. xxii:1.

In this discourse we shall more fully show why "a good name is rather to be chosen than great riches."

Though wealth is desirable, and in many instances conducive to human happiness, because it puts it in our power to relieve the wants and distresses of our fellow creatures, yet it does not possess the charm to convey unbroken peace or solid joy to any bosom. The value, of anything within the range of human action, is to be estimated by its usefulness in promoting the happiness of man. That, which pours the most numerous and refined enjoyments into the soul, is to be considered of the greatest worth; and that, which has a tendency to bring upon us the most alarming miseries, misfortunes and woes, is of course the most worthless. The one is to be fondly chosen and pursued in proportion to its worth in administering to our enjoyments, and the other is to be avoided in proportion to its unhappy effects in multiplying our sorrows. This being an undeniable fact, the superlative value of a good name, procured by a virtuous course of conduct, appears, at once, to transcend all other considerations: A pure unsullied conscience before heaven is the most permanent bliss that a rational being can enjoy, and is of that enduring nature which no earthly power or misfortune can destroy. It supports us in the hour of adversity and trial; it comforts us in the dark hour of sorrow; it remains unmoved amids the storms of life, and lights up the smile of satisfaction on the lips of the dying.

Nor is this all. It affords us other unruffled streams of unmingled felicity in the common intercourse of life. The approbation of the wise and the good, the confidence and esteem of our friends and associates, and the good opinion even of the vicious, are considerations of no ordinary moment. They awaken emotions in the heart of the most pleasing gratification, and open in the soul all the avenues of heaven-born felicity, imparting that peace, which this world can neither give nor take away. But as it respects *wealth*, we would remark, that though it may communicate happiness by enabling us to relieve the wants of our fellow creatures, and afford us many joys in the indulgence of our benevolence, yet it cannot of itself communicate happiness, but virtue can. A wicked and unprincipled man is wretched, though he roll in all the wealth and splendors that earth can give. He feels in his bosom a *burning flame*, that all the streams of wealth can never quench, and a *craving desire*, that nought on earth can gratify. If his "great riches" afford him any enjoyments, yet these are by no means permanent and lasting. The desolating flame may lay them in ruins—the storms on the ocean may sink them in its waves—the famine or blighting mildew may wither them forever, and leave him stript of all his fancied joys. But nothing of this can happen to virtue. That remains forever unharmed amidst the shocks of earth. A good name is, therefore, of inconceivably more value than riches and rather to be chosen than silver and gold.

We are formed for society. God in beginning said, "it is not good that man should be alone." This being a fact, which all past experience, and the history of our whole race demonstrate, it is, therefore, equally true, that our dearest enjoyments flow from the social affections and from a sincere cultivation of the social intercourse of life. There is, perhaps, not a human being in existence, who would accept of all the wealth of the Indies on the condition that he should not be respected by a single individual on earth. This circumstance shows us, in noonday light, the superior value of a good name above all the glittering appendages of wealth. Every man is beloved and esteemed in proportion to his goodness and usefulness in the world, particularly by those with whom he associate in life. If then to *love and be beloved* depend on our conduct in the world, and if at the same time, our happiness is derived from the exercise of reciprocal affection, we see the importance of pitching upon that course of life, which alone can secure those solid pleasures resulting from a well spent life.

Too many persons suppose, they can be happy in sin; yes, even in criminal indulgence. But that transgressor was never yet found, who could point to a single wicked act in his life, the remembrance of which ever imparted one solitary gleam of joy to his heart. They may fancy there is happiness in sin; but here is the deception. It is immaterial what some may preach about *the pleasures of sin*, and *the satisfaction the transgressor often takes in a wicked course*, yet all this amounts to nothing so long as the voice of heaven declares, "THERE IS NO PEACE, SAITH MY GOD, TO THE WICKED." Infinite wisdom *must know*, and infinite wisdom, *has given* the decision, and that decision is stamped with immortality, and from it there is no appeal. If we impress the sinner with the idea that he is not punished and rewarded *here*, but that the whole is to be settled in the future world, then we, in the same proportion, weaken the force of virtue and *strengthen* the cause of vice. And this is one obvious reason, why men continue in sin, as long as they dare, expecting at some future day to repent and escape *all punishment*. They go on from day to day, and from year to year, with all the thunders of endless and immortal pain sounded in their ears, and even believing it true, yet continue to indulge in sin. Would they run such an awful risk, unless, by a certain course of education, they had been made to believe that there was happiness in transgression? No. If they believed that sin had nought to impart but misery, they would abandon it for its *own sake*; because happiness is the object of all men. They have, therefore, by some means or other, been led to the strange infatuation, that sin possesses some secret charm to communicate that happiness to the soul, for which every bosom throbs. This fancied happiness, they vainly imagine, they can obtain by wallowing in the dark waters of iniquity, be happy *here*, then repent at last, and be happy *hereafter*. As they pass along in their wretched career, expecting every moment to grasp the fancied pleasure, yet the fond, anticipated phantom flies from their embrace and leaves them in the ruin of their joy. Though disappointed again and again, yet firmly believing that there is happiness in sin, they again push on, and thus far attribute their want of success to some miscalculation. Insensible of the nature of sin, blinded and self-deceived, they go on in pursuit of pleasure, while golden dreams of false felicity fire their imaginations, till at last, age places them on the verge of the grave; their object no nearer attained than it was the day they set out, while habit has fixed them in a course, that has yielded them nothing but sorrow and pain, and vanity and vexation of spirit. Stung with remorse, and pierced through with many sorrows, they breathe a repentance, which, the nature of their condition, forces upon them, are perhaps pronounced *converted*, and they sink into the darkness of death! Their names, covered with infamy, are soon blotted from the remembrance of the living!

We observed, a moment ago, that the idea, of holding up a retribution in the future world, weakens the force of virtue, and strengthens the cause of vice. This has, perhaps, been abundantly shown in the arguments already offered as being manifest in the daily conduct of men; yet we will, in a word, bring the subject plainly before you. To persuade a sinner that he is to be punished in the *future* world for his sins in *this*, is plainly saying that sin has many pleasures and conveniences *here*, and so far as it failed of rendering him his due desert, the balance is to be made up in another state of being. Because the balance of punishment due him *there*, is to make up the *deficiency* of punishment, which sin did not pay him here. And certainly, so far as sin did not pay him *here*, he must have been happy in its commission. And the *expectation*, that he should be happy in it *here*, was the *very cause* that induced him to continue in transgression, with the expectation of repenting and escaping punishment *hereafter*. Thus he flattered himself, that he could sin with impunity, and escape its punishment in this world and the world to come.

And to satisfy a man that he is to be rewarded in the *future* world for his righteousness in *this* but persuading him, that virtue is attended with misery, and that so far as it failed to reward *here*, the balance is to be made up *hereafter*. Because the balance of happiness due to him *there*, is to make up the deficiency of happiness which virtue did not pay him *here*. And so far as virtue did not pay him here, must have been miserable in its practice. And the impression that sin is productive of many enjoyments, and that righteousness is attended with misery, has a tendency to make him choose the *former* and reject the *latter*, and trust to a future repentance.

We often hear it proclaimed by those, who profess to be the guardians of the public morals, that the righteous have a hard course in warring against the corruptions of their heart, in the service of God, while the sinner goes on unconcerned and easy in the pleasures of sin. In doing this they defeat the very object, they are striving to obtain, which is the *conversion* of the sinner. These very impressions are one obvious reason why so many continue in sin and reject the path of righteousness and peace, which alone conducts to a good name, that is of more worth than great riches, and more durable than silver and gold.

As then there is no happiness in vice, as all its allurements are deceptive and vain, how important that we should shun it, and pursue that bright path of virtue and peace, which will lead to the invaluable possession of a good name. Engaging in the cultivation of all the better affections of the heart, we shall by habit so refine our natures, that "loving favor" will take entire possession of our minds, and mould them into the spotless image of heaven. *This* loving favor is rather to be chosen than silver and gold, for these will corrupt, and at last crumble into dust, while *this* shall survive the ruins of death, and flourish in those peaceful realms, where our felicity will be unbroken and perpetual.

Flatter not yourselves with the vain hope, that there is one solitary thrill of joy in the indulgence of sin. He, who indulges in dissipation and vice—he, who slanders his neighbor, who wrongs his fellow men, or even utters one oath against the unsullied name of his Maker, is a most profound unbeliever in the sentiment we proclaim. He, who possesses a hope so full of immortality as to believe, that God will finally save from sin, and bless him and all his fellow men, will cleanse his hands and wash them in innocency. Tell me not that you are a Universalist, when the very oceans of God's goodness do not affect your heart, nor lead you to repentance. He, who is satisfied that there is no happiness in sin, will abandon it. He, who deliberately pursues a vicious course, expects to find happiness in it; and it is impossible that he believes in God's *universal grace*. It is absolutely impossible in the very nature of things, that he can be a UNIVERSALIST. A salvation from sin is the doctrine of the Bible, and holiness itself heaven. He, who believes such a salvation to be happifying, will abandon sin, as the enemy of his peace, and seek righteousness, which alone can afford him tranquillity. Jesus says, the kingdom of heaven is righteousness and peace. If you wish to satisfy men that you *really* desire the whole human family to meet in heaven, then show your sincerity by being righteous yourself.

A sincere Universalist believes sin to be the cause of many mental woes that darken the world, and the principal cause of the greater proportion of sufferings that fall to the lot of man. He believes that a virtuous course of conduct, guided by the burning lamp of revelation, leads to those joys that time cannot sully, nor the hand of death extinguish. A conviction of this truth leads him to hate sin, to forsake its dark dominions, and enter those fields of felicity, where the brilliant beams of virtue shed a cloudless day. Here he walks and enjoys an antepast of heaven. Its paths are the paths of peace. All its ways are pleasantness and delight. Its crystal streams are pure and sweet; its breezes healthful and its fruits delicious. He believes God to be the father of his creatures—that he governs the world in wisdom and mercy—that he created with a benevolent intention, and that he is not disappointed in the workmanship of his hand, but presides over just such a world as he designed it should be. He believes that this order of things, though dark to him, is designed for good, and shall terminate in the happiness of all. He believes that all rewards and punishments are instituted for some benevolent end, and that this end, will be brought about in such a manner as to manifest to all, the divine perfections in the clearest light, and shed unfading glory on the supreme Majesty of heaven. This faith gives him confidence in his heavenly Father, and fills his heart with gratitude and veneration. It leads him to look upon the human family as his brethren, and to do them good. He seeks their happiness, and thus chooses and merits a good name.

At peace with all mankind, his mind irradiated with light and enlarged with the most noble conceptions of the divine character and government, bout, he at length lies down in peace and composure upon his dying bed, and gently breathes out—

"Farewell conflicting joys and fears,
Where light and shade alternatedwell;
A brighter, purer scene appears,
Farewell inconstant world, farewell!"

He sweetly sinks to rest, and leaves behind him a good name, that can never die, and an example, for others to imitate, worth more than fortunes in gold. His memory shall survive, when the tomb, on which it is inscribed, shall crumble into ruin, and his example be a light to future generations.

SERMON XIV

"Be of the same mind one towards another. Mind not high things, but condescend to men of low estate." Romans xii. 16.

That mysterious and incomprehensible Being, who gave us existence, has sown in our nature the seeds of mortality. By the irresistible *laws* of his empire which he has, from the beginning, *established* for the regulating of the animal creation, we are soon to be carried to the silent grave. All, without exception, are formed out of equal clay, are subject to the same hopes and fears, joys and sorrows while on earth, and are all destined to the slumbers of death, where we must exhibit the emblem of perfect equality. Immaterial how far one may exalt himself above another while passing through this momentary existence—immaterial how far he may rise above his fellow men in the scale of intellect and refinement—immaterial how exalted the station he may have obtained—how brilliant the powers of his imagination may sparkle, or how soft and sublime his eloquence may flow—immaterial how nobly soever he may dazzle in the sunny smiles of fortune, or how secure he may repose in the fond embrace of friends, yet it is a melancholy truth, that he must, sooner or later, resign the whole, let go his eager grasp on all those pleasing joys, bid an everlasting farewell to those exalted splendors, and descend to the dark shades of death, where the rich and the poor, the servant and his master, the oppressor and oppressed, all lie mouldering and forgotten together.

This solemn consideration, it seems, when forcibly presented to the mind, ought to be sufficient to check the levity of man—to soften his bosom to his fellow beings—to moderate his desire in pursuit of wealth and greatness, and completely to unarm him of all hostile feelings towards those with whom he associates, and with whom he is so soon to lie down in death. This, it seems, is sufficient to make us of one heart and mind in promoting each other's happiness and welfare in the world, and to make us obedient to the exhortation of the text, not to mind the high things of earth, but to condescend to men of low estate. But such is the strange infatuation of man, that he acts as though his residence on earth were eternal, and as though the whole errand of life consisted in providing for an eternity below.

We are capacitated for enjoyments of a higher and more perfect nature than we can attain to on earth. Of this we are sensible from the fact, that there is no condition in which we can be placed here below, that is so adapted to our nature as to afford us permanent satisfaction. Uninterrupted felicity is not a plant of earth. It cannot flourish in a clime where the blighting storms of malice and envy wither all that is fair, sweet and blooming. And though we are sensible that such is the fact, yet, deaf to all that experience, example and observation conspire to teach, we are exerting all our powers to obtain it here below, where the united voice of earth and heaven assure us it cannot be found. We cast our eyes around us, and see the human family in every varied condition of life from the beggar on his bed of straw, up to the king in regal splendor on the throne of nations; but in defiance of this immense distinction, they alike breathe the deep sigh of discontent. We also cast our eyes over the historic page, and scan the general fate of man in by-gone ages; but here too, we learn the same lesson, that no *external condition* has ever added to the rational enjoyments of the soul. We see the same uneasiness, the same longing desires pervade every bosom. Our object is happiness; and amidst all the various pursuits of life, what is the reason so many fail of obtaining it? The answer is readily given. We make riches, honors and the high things of the earth our chief pursuit and aim, and fondly imagine that our happiness lies in them. Here is our error. Man is destined to a world of mental felicity, where those external pursuits of fortune will be unknown; where all that he here pursues with so much eagerness will be removed from his desires forever, and where all the channels of the soul will be opened to the true fountain of felicity and completely ravished in its flowing streams. In order, therefore, to enjoy that happiness, in this momentary state of being, which God has placed within our reach, we must make mental felcity the main pursuit of life, and the riches and conveniences of earth our secondary pursuit. We must completely reverse our conduct in order to obtain those rational enjoyments, that flow from the virtuous habits and dispositions. We must, as Jesus says, "seek first the kingdom of God and his righteousness and all these things shall be added unto you."

Food and raiment are all that we can enjoy of the external comforts of life. All other enjoyments must be of a mental character. Secure first your mental joys, a pure unsullied conscience in the punctual discharge of all your social and relative duties to mankind, and be you rich or poor, you will be happy. The righteous discharge of this first great duty will not embarrass you in obtaining the comforts of life, but on the contrary aid you. A peaceable and honest course of conduct towards others—a condescension to men of low estate—a due respect for the opinions and rights of others, will endear you to all, and not only foster in your bosom the seeds of peace and contentment, but will conduct you in the surest path to wealth and honor. The mental powers of the soul are all that exalt our capacity for happiness above a brutal creation. And if our chief happiness lies in gold, which can only minister to our animal wants, then the brutes can vie with us in all the solid enjoyments of life. In fact, they can go beyond us. They graze the turf, and drink the unmingled stream free from anxiety and care. While man, the lord of this lower creation, has to toil and gain the same enjoyments by the sweat of his brow.

But what a groveling thought to bring our exalted natures and capacities for happiness down to a level with theirs! On this principle, he who is the most wealthy is the most happy. Virtue is but a name, and all the exalted principles of noble and godlike action are but the reveries of fancy, and to practice them is but a visionary dream. No, my friends, wealth supplies our animal wants, and if virtue be wanting, it leaves our minds in wretched starvation and our brightest joys in night! Happiness is equally attainable by the rich and the poor. It consists in a union of heart among mankind, in a union of action in the pursuit of virtue, and in the kindlier feelings of our nature. In fine, it consists in a willing obedience to the exhortations of our text: "Be of the same mind one towards another. Mind not high things, but condescend to men of low estate."

To each of these exhortations, we will give a candid and solemn consideration. In this sermon, we will attend to the exhortation—"*Be of the same mind one towards another.*" By this, we are not to understand that men are to be of one heart and mind in pursuing the same occupation or profession in life, but of one mind in endeavoring to promote each other's happiness in every condition in which they may be placed—of one mind in the practice of christian duty, and in the exercise of charity. Selfishness produces many jarring interests among mankind, bursts the bands of brotherhood asunder, and weakens the strength of that nation, society or family among which it exists, and in proportion to the opposition it produces among its individual members. "United, we stand, divided we fall," is a maxim full of wisdom, and is not only applicable to nations, but to communities, societies, and even to families.

A family in discord is a sight over which angels might weep, but when united in one heart and mind, it is a picture over which heaven smiles. The fond and doating father, the tender and affectionate mother, and obedient children, all united in peace and harmony, present to the mind those pleasing conceptions of the reconciled family immortal, that cause us to feel all the burning emotions of which the heart is susceptible. In such society as this, are enjoyed the happiest moments of our existence—moments unmingled with the bitterness of regret, unsullied by the corroding hand of time, unruffled by the perplexing cares of life, and undarkened by the tempests of indisposition. Is such a father absent—far distant on land or ocean where duty calls? The heart of his family goes with him, and he too leaves his heart lingering behind. His companion counts the moments as they slowly roll—is faithful to his interests—makes preparation to receive him—sighs for his safe return, and welcomes him home with those emotions of ecstatic joy, that cause him to forget his past labors, toils and dangers. Is he stretched upon a bed of pain? Unwearied she sits beside him, hushes every sound that might interrupt his broken slumbers, and watches every breath he draws. She whispers to him the soothing words of encouragement and consolation— gives neither sleep to her eyes, nor slumber to her eyelids, but is the guardian angel of his pillow.

When all human aid has failed—when the pulse beats faint—the once sparkling eye grows dim and rolls faint and languid in its socket, she stands mute and pensive at his dying bed. Her whole soul is absorbed in the interest of the scene and rent with agony. She wipes the cold sweat of death from his face, gazes with exquisite anxiety till the last dreadlful struggle is over, and breathes to the throne of mercy the prayer of affection for the repose of his spirit. And so feels the kind husband over his companion, indulgent parents over their dying children, and dutiful children over their parents.

But it is a lamentable circumstance, a painful consideration, that there are too many unhappy divisions in the domestic circle. Yes, it is a painful consideration indeed, that those, who are so nearly allied to each other, should, even for one moment, indulge in feelings of acrimony. It is but a short time, at longest, that we can be together, and such unhappy divisions must render the parting scene, at the bed of death, doubly painful. Thoughtless, giddy or oppressive as we may be to those, who are near to us in life, while blooming health is their lot, yet righteous heaven has so constituted our natures, that the most painful reminiscences will force themselves upon the mind when the injured object, to whom we have given distress, is upon a dying bed. Every unkind word, every harsh treatment, the whole dark picture our ungenerous conduct will present itself to the imagination in all its naked woes. And be that dying one a parent, a companion, a child, their very silence, as thy turn upon us a languid eye fading in death, will harrow up every painful recollection. O! if we wish to tread upon their graves with an unsullied conscience before heaven, let us be of one mind, live in peace, and discharge, to them, those sacred duties of kindness and affection, which the ties, that bind them to us, enjoin.

This world is too much made up of appearances. Many a family, which we suppose to be the abode of union, peace and joy, is distracted with the voice of discord, and is dragging out an existence in secret, concealed grief. Many a husband and wife, who, we suppose, are of one heart and mind and passing their days in the sunshine of peace and love, are torn by secret broils, and whose mansion stands overcast with the dark shadows of discontent and misery. Little do we dream of the secret woes, that rend many a worthy heart concealed behind a smiling countenance. The husband is perhaps stern and unrelenting—and will, in no case, yield to the wishes of his companion. Discouragement and anger may perhaps at times take possession of the heart. In such a case, instead of treating her kindly, he rouses into a passion himself, and a private contention ensues. This is a wretched practice, for instead of extinguishing the flame, it adds fuel to the fire, and consumes all that is fair and lovely in matrimonial and domestic life. Much misery might be avoided by observing the following rule. When the one is melancholy, let the other be rationally cheerful, and endeavor to divert the attention from the subject that causes gloom. When the one is angry, let the other keep a perfect equanimity and a benign composure of countenance. Then watch the opportunity, and in some future day, when the offended one is most cheerful and kind, then bring forward the subject, and expostulate most feelingly on the impropriety of indulging a wrathful spirit to a bosom friend. Speak of the shortness of life and point each other to the silent grave and to the parting scene, and vengeance, anger and discontent will soon be strangers in your habitation. Your dear children, from the very dawnings of intellect, will take the example, grow up in harmony and affection with perfect rule over their spirit, and thus you will not only secure your own domestic peace, but will bequeath those sacred enjoyments to your posterity—enjoyments that infinitely outweigh a thousand fortunes in gold! Let others toil to leave their offspring wealth, we ours the joy to bequeath them this. We ask no more.

We are not only to be of the same mind one towards another in our families but in our religious societies. Here all selfishness ought to be discarded, all private interests sacrificed, all hostile feelings subdued, and the whole offered on the altar of genuine good, and thus the harmony, peace and prosperity of the whole body consulted. The permanent security of these depend on the individual conduct of the members. By uniting ourselves in a religious body, we express the necessity of living a sober life, maintaining a union of heart and a respectful conversation towards all with whom we associate in life. Let us not dream that heaven will prosper us above others, if we also blaspheme the name of Him who gave us life and sustains us in being. Let us lay aside every evil, that has a tendency to disunion, and live soberly and righteously in the world, doing good unto all as we have opportunity.

[The reader will find this subject continued in our next number.]

SERMON XV

"Be of the same mind one towards another. Mind not high things, but condescend to men of low estate." Romans xii. 16.

Having from the commencement of these sermons confined myself to prescribed limits, I had no room in my last to pursue the first division of my subject so far as I intended. I will therefore here resume it.

"*Be of the same mind, one towards another.*" We have thus far confined our attention to family union, and have just glanced at the necessity of union in religious societies. This is a day of inquiry and light when the most keen and searching glances are sent into every creed. Many denominations that have walked together heart and hand for many years, each repelling the assaults of those, who attempted to extinguish their ism, have at length been separated by internal divisions and formed two opposing parties, even though they once believed the *same creed*, and advocated the *same church government*. The present is a trying period, and it stands us in hand to endeavor to "keep the unity of the spirit in the bonds of peace." Let us not dream of religious union, and prosperity, unless we allow each one to think for himself in matters of scripture interpretation. Nor let us dream of prosperity, if there is among us more theory than practice. It is true, Universalists are as moral as any other denomination; but this is not enough. They ought in *kindness and benevolence* to transcend other denominations as far, as their doctrine of universal beniguity transcends the doctrine of unending wo.

Neither are we to dream of religious union and prosperity, unless we raise our united voices against those who revel over the flowing cup of intoxication, which pours so many streams of misery and disunion on the world. Let no one fancy to himself that the drunkards toast, "*here is health and success to us!*" has any charm to avert his ruin, or to stay the judgment of heaven. The more frequently that toast has been uttered, while smiling upon the cup of inebriation held in a trembling hand, the farther have health and success been removed from the deluded victim, and the more swift and deadly have misfortune, sickness, distress and pain fallen upon him. Intemperance is a demon, that sows the seeds of discord among all ranks, orders and conditions of men. Beneath his crushing hand creation reels, and fortunes fall in broken ruins! And peace the sweet angel of mercy flies these turbulent skies, and lights on realms unmoved by the hand of commotion and discord. At his approach, blooming health is driven back from its warm abode and the fairest flowers of domestic love, hope and joy are withered forever! Let this frightful foe of discord and confusion be barred from our sacred heritage and peace be within our borders.

We are not only to be of one heart and one mind in resisting profanity and intemperance, but in resisting tale-bearing. Let us not speak evil of others. This is beneath the character of a gentleman, and certainly beneath that of a christian: consequently no gentleman or christian will indulge in it. It is the employment of *low, ill-bred minds*, and therefore none will engage in it, but those who are destitute of reputation themselves. This vice has no excuse, and must therefore originate in the *basest* motives. They intend to bring their fellow creatures down to a level with themselves, and thus lessen them in the good opinion of others, and destroy their peace. And though they may effect their object so far as the good opinion of the virtuous is calculated to give us happiness, yet the approbation of a good conscience, arising from the conviction of innocency, can never he rooted from the heart of its possessor by all the calumnies of earth. *This* God has secured in all the secret chambers of the soul, and forever barred it against the breath of slander. There he takes up his abode and holds communion with the contrite spirit. The real merits and consolations of virtue are secured to its possessor by the impartial legislation of righteous heaven. Intemperance in its effects, compared with slandering, is harmless; at least so far as producing discord is concerned. The peaceable drunkard, compared even with that church member, who is continually sowing discord in society, is an angel. Slander is but the infectious breath or a foul spirit, that poisons the healthful atmosphere wherever it is breathed, and breaks the quiet repose—the calm serenity of neighborhoods and families, as it were, with an electric shock.

Political slander is as infectious and destructive to the harmony of the nation, and the security of our government, as private slander is to neighborhoods and societies. No sooner is a candidate held up for office, than all the party dogs of war on both sides are let loose and set to barking. Immaterial how fair may be his character, how inviolable his veracity, or how unsullied his honor and integrity, they will make him appear to be an outcast from society, covered with the darkest blots of infamy. Immaterial how great may be his qualifications, or how splendid his talents, they will, by that species of logic for which slanderers are famous, prove him to be a fool. These dissentions do not expire when the candidates are elected. They are carried to the capitol of our common country and blown out in more than wordy war. There, we have reason to fear, the volcano is gathering, and that the day is not distant when it will disembogue in more than the thunders of Etna, wrap our political heavens in a blaze, and melt its elements with fervent heat. Anarchy and confusion will seize the reins of government, and drive us to the oblivious shades of departed empires. If we continue to go on in our political slanders as a nation, losing sight of our common welfare, and sacrificing the *general*, on the altar of *partial* interest, the day of our ruin is not remote. Its awful morn, has, already, it seems, dawned with streaks of malignant *light*, and (like ill fated Troy) ominous of the purple streams, the crimson blood, that watered the Trojan plains where mighty Sarpedon fell, where Hector lay slain by the sword of Achilles. Heaven forbid that our national sun, that rose so fair, should go down in blood, and shroud our temple of Liberty in everlasting night! To avert such a catastrophe let us reform, and do our duty as individuals. The safety of any body politic depends on the conduct of the individuals that compose it. And God grant that these dissentions may cease, that political peace and harmony may become perfect, and our government may stand immoveable on its basis, like the rock that remains unshaken by the furious storms that agitate the ocean. May we, as a nation, be of one mind in resisting every species of immorality, in studying the happiness of our fellow creatures—of one mind in obtaining a knowledge of the character of our Creator, in studying his parental and benign government, and his divine attributes and unchanging perfections—and be of one mind in acquainting ourselves with his beautiful works that swarm around us and afford us so many rational delights. Let us store our minds with useful knowledge, practice the precept of Christ, labor for mental emancipation, and contentment and peace will be our lot.

In the great duties of religious obligation, let us be of one heart and mind. Let us live like brethren, not only among ourselves, but among other denominations. It is not long that we are to be together. We are fading like the flower of the field, and ought to bear in mind that death will soon lay our heads equally low in the dust, and the worms shall cover us. We glitter for a moment like the bubbles borne on the bosom of the ocean; they break and mingle again with the parent fountain. We toil and heap up wealth, pass like empty shadows over the plain and vanish forever! Generations, that covered the earth, are gone, and unremembered by the living. They strove to gather wealth and honors—they met each other in the hostile field—rolled garments in blood, bedewed the widow's and the orphan's cheek with tears, and filled their peaceful habitations with the voice of lamentation and wo. Thousands lived in clamors and discord, and one seemed destined to be oppressed by another. But the fields of war are still, the noise of battle is hushed, and the voice of lamentation and wo is heard no more! Hark! All is still as the chambers of eternal silence! Where are they? In the shades of death! Kind reader, this is the doom of us all! And so it will soon be said of you and me! Let us then be of one mind. Let us do good by visiting the fatherless in their affliction and keeping ourselves unspotted from the world.

We have now considered the fact, that real felicity consists in mental pleasures and gratifications, and that these alone exalt our nature and capacity for happiness above the brute creation, and have directed your attention to virtue and peace as the only condition in which that happiness can be found. We have brought to view the propriety of being of one heart and mind towards each other in our families, in our religious societies, in the community and in our national concerns. We have set before you the evils resulting from intemperance, and from private and political slander.

We will now, in the *second* place, take into consideration the *negative and affirmative* consequence resulting from them on the morals of the community so far as the causes leading to *intemperance and crime* are concerned.

Many discourses have been delivered, during the three past years, on intemperance pointing out its ruinous effects on the morals of society, while but few discourses have been put into the hands of the public pointing out the causes leading to this destructful vice, and those few have not in my humble opinion traced it to its *true source*. Much has also been said about intemperance leading to crime, which in many respects is true. But all this is not coming to the fountainhead from whence these turbid streams flow. We will take the liberty to differ on this subject with all that has as yet fallen upon our ear, and independently give our opinion, as to what we conceive to be the original cause from whence these baneful effects spring. We will endeavor to show that *the poorer class of society are driven to intemperance and crime by the conduct of the rich (those whom the fashion of the world calls respectable and great) yes, by the conduct of too many, who are even attempting to reform them.*

First, then we would remark; that man is a creature of want, which is the first cause of all action. Had he no wants, he would never seek to supply them, either by *honorable or dishonorable* means. To this self-evident proposition, all will without hesitation assent. We will now attend to our general character as a nation, for it will be admitted, on all hands, that actions speak louder than words. As a nation, we enjoy much liberty; but public opinion, either of a political or religious character, may become so popular as to erect itself into an engine of oppression, and so formidable, that many an honest man dare not dissent, nor independently raise his voice in defence of what he believes to be truth, but will tamely submit himself a slave to the opinions and doctrines of others. This is probably the case with the greater proportion of the American people.

Again, though we profess to value every man by his integrity or moral worth, yet it is a fact, that in conduct we make a man's reputation depend principally on his purse. I yield the point without controversy that in books, in newspapers, in preaching and in words, we profess to esteem a man and rate his standing in society by his integrity. But what do words and books, and newspapers and preaching amount to, while mankind in conduct practice right the contrary of all these ostentatious professions? They amount to nothing but hypocrisy, or ridiculous nonsense. Does a man's standing, in these days, depend on his conduct! By no means. Let us introduce an example. Suppose there were two individuals of equal talents, and both possessed an equal education. Their moral characters are the same. But one of them falls in possession of an immense fortune, while the other is poor indeed. Now will public conduct place them on an equality? No. Will they both move in the same social circle? No. Will they both be treated with the same politeness and attention by their neighbors? No. Should they propose a public measure for the good of the town, would the one be listened to, with the same attention as the other? No. Would he possess so much influence in society? No. Well, what can be assigned as the reason, why this rich man stands so far above the other in the public opinion? Ans. It is because his character is measured by the length of his purse, and the weight of his influence is determined by the weight of his gold.

It is not a thing of rare occurrence, that the rich are thus distinguished from the poor, but it is a fact so notorious that it has long since passed into a proverb. This being the course of conduct which men practice, the impression has therefore become general that reputation, influence and power depend on wealth. Hence the great inquiry, uppermost in every mind, is "how shall I get rich, so that I may stand high in the estimation of men, and exert a powerful influence in society, and be numbered among those who move in the higher circles of life?" Concluded in our next.

SERMON XVI

"Be of the same mind one towards another. Mind not high things, but condescend to men of low estate." Romans xii:12.

Even a man, who is in many things unprincipled, if he is at the same time wealthy, takes a station in the higher circles of life, where the poor, but honest man, would not be admitted. This course of conduct is not only practised by what are called men of the world, but by professors of religion of about all denominations, by both preachers and people.

The middling, and the poor class, seeing no encouragement, or even possibility, of rising so as to associate with those, who move in the higher circles of life, by any virtuous conduct they may pursue, and sensible that wealth alone possesses the charm to give them virtue and notice in the world, they are thus driven to various, dishonorable means to obtain it. Multitudes are driven to the crimes of counterfeiting, theft, and even robbery and piracy. They commence their wretched course, with the intention to abandon it, as soon as a competent fortune is obtained. Other thousands are driven to gambling; and even those, who are called respectable, take every possible advantage in trade and bargaining. Their pursuits are various, but their object is one and the same—viz: to gain wealth, so that they may obtain a high standing and influence in society. Thousands thus driven into crime, are detected, lose their reputation, and abandon themselves to intemperance. Their evil example has a pernicious influence on the morals of those children and youth, who may, by various circumstances, be placed in their society, and thus the pestilence, in all its frightful horrors, gathers force and spreads.

There are thousands of virtuous persons, whom poverty excludes from the higher ranks of life, who are doomed to seek the converse of those, who are in a measure corrupted, and, by associating with them on public occasions, often in taverns and alehouses, are soon involved in habits of dissipation and obscenity. Man is a social being, loves society, and, rather than spend his life in solitude, will seek the converse of the vicious.

If we would obey the injunction of the text—"Mind not high things, but condescend to men of low estate," these evils would be in a great measure removed. If we, as a community, would strip away the fancied reputation, which wealth attaches to the human character, and, independent of property, place every man on an equal footing, according to their moral and mental worth, and let their power and influence in society, be according to their conduct, it would give a noble tone to public feeling and moral grandeur.

By the "*high things*," mentioned in our text, we are to understand that vain popularity which one man wishes to enjoy above another, in a religious or political sense. It is one of the ruling passions of the day, in which we live, to be considered of high standing among our fellow creatures, and to possess a larger share of influence over the minds and opinions of men, than those whom we consider our rivals. Those, who possess this desire, and at the same time feel a haughty spirit towards those, whom they consider in the humble walks of life, are certainly not the men, who are entitled to our esteem, nor are they to be looked up to, as examples of magnanimity. So far from possessing true greatness of soul, or being entitled to veneration, they are certainly below those whom they affect to despise. A truly great and good man has no desire to dazzle, but to be useful in the world. He sees the miseries under which thousands groan, and desires to relieve them, but with no wish to be considered great for discharging those duties of kindness and humanity. But it is a lamentable consideration, that too many, in performing those acts of mercy, seek to stand on an eminence above the crowd they wish to benefit, and proclaim their intentions to men through the loud sounding trumpet of fame, but, at the same time, will not even stoop to converse with the very beings they profess such a warm desire to aid. Every thing must be done on a high scale, and in the manner they dictate, otherwise they have no wish it should be done at all. It is a matter of regret, that this spirit, so desirous of minding high things, has been carried into the sanctuary—in fact, has been carried to the solemn gates of death—yes, even into eternity.

We have witnessed what are commonly called "revivals of religion," in which two or more denominations united, apparently, heart and hand. They publicly declared, that as they saw their fellow creatures exposed to the burning wrath of God in the future world, they had no motive in view, but their conversion and escape from that awful doom— that it was, to them, a matter of indifference with what church they united themselves, provided, they would only repent and turn to God. All this passed on well till the reformation ceased. The next thing, to be determined, was, what doctrine do you believe, and what church will you join? This was a trying point, and its settlement filled them with animosity towards each other. And why? Because each desired the honor of converting them to their faith, and of bringing them into their church, or else, that they should not be converted at all. Though this has been done by some, yet it is no evidence, that all will do this, or even approve it. There are those, who, we believe, are actuated by nobler motives than in the cause of truth, and who are not aspiring to stand high, nor striving "who shall be greatest." One denomination has labored to assume the entire honor of reforming the public morals—has labored to become incorporated by an act of Legislature into an American Temperance Society, and were unwilling to admit Universalists and Unitarians to co-operate with them in this work of reform. This is but aspiring after high things, instead of manifesting the meek and lowly spirit of Christ.

But we would more particularly remark that, it is this very course of conduct of any man, or class of men exalting themselves above others in account of their *wealth, or external circumstances,* that discourages the poor, who are not only called, but treated as the lower order of society, and drives thousands of them to the intoxicating cup, as a relief from the mortifications of poverty, and drives other thousands into crime, as the only means to obtain that wealth by the omnipotence of which, they alone can rise to eminence, respectability, and influence among men. Preachers of the gospel, as well as others, give sanction by their conduct to these false notions of respectability and greatness. They will seek the society, and court the favor of the rich in preference to the poor, even though the *latter* may exceed the *former* in integrity and moral worth. This, we say, is the most powerful incentive to drive men into a state of encouragement, intemperance and crime. It is a fearful precipice on which we stand, as a religious community. Instead of estimating a man's standing by his virtuous principles, it is too much estimated by his dollars.

So did not Jesus Christ our great example. He mingled with the lowest class of society. He associated with, and visited most among those he wished to reform, so that his meek, mild and heavenly example might exert a salutary influence upon their hearts, and cast a restraint upon their conduct. He was a friend to publicans and sinners, and ate and drank with them. He went among them, as a physician, to give them life and health, to conduct them by encouragement and persuasion to the paths of righteousness and peace. His presence was not needed among those who were whole. He was of course seldom found in their society. He did not desire to rank with the rich, self-righteous pharisee. So ought those, who profess to be the servants of Christ, to go among them, who are most in need of their aid. "The servant is not above his Master." They ought, therefore, to condescend to men of low estate, and visit the abodes of poverty and want.

But instead of this, they stand aloof, even from the respectable, because they are poor, and instead of visiting those, who indulge in dissipation and vice, and trying to lead them to the paths of virtue and peace, are heaping upon them the most opprobrious epithets. By esteeming the rich and associating with them, they practice a course of conduct, which has rooted the impression deep in every mind, that to be esteemed, and to rank with them in the social circle, they must be rich. This has driven many a virtuous man into crime, many into bad company, and finally into discouragement and intoxication. This no one can deny. What, we ask, is the reason, that there is so large a proportion of the middle and lower class of society, compared with the rich, who indulge in *crimes and intemperance*? Why is it when misfortune falls upon the rich, that they, so often, resort to the intoxicating draught? The mystery can only be unriddled in the stubborn fact, that wealth, more than virtue, gives a man a reputation in the world, and this destructive vice involves thousands in ruin.

If every man were assured that, be he *rich or poor*, he could associate with those who are wealthy and respected, and move in the higher ranks of life, if he only maintained his integrity, and that he would be esteemed in proportion to his moral virtues and mental acquirements, every man would be induced to merit a good name; and their good opinion would operate as a constant check upon his conduct. Every man, by early attention to his deportment, can become respectable, but every man cannot become wealthy.

Did the rich esteem the poor, and admit them into their social circle *solely* on the ground of moral worth, there would be but little danger of these poor ever forfeiting their standing, by plunging into the floods of intemperance and crime. And did they reject from their circle the rich, who were vicious until reformed—in fine, did they only strip away from wealth its fancied charm, to make them either respectable, or influential, did they confine it to its due limits, as being only necessary to satisfy our animal wants, and did they with one consent declare that an improved mind and virtuous worth should be the only criterion by which men should take their stations in social life, intemperance and crime would soon cease. Men would then be as much engaged in striving to merit a fair reputation, as they are how in striving to obtain wealth. It is, therefore, the conduct of the great by falsely attaching character and influence to wealth, that is driving their fellow creatures into crimes to obtain it, and other thousands into discouragement and intemperance. From this charge preachers are not exempt. They too respect, and visit the rich more than the poor, and thus indirectly lend their influence to drive them from virtuous life to a course of dissipation and crime. And when once they get them there, then they wish to devise some *great means* to bring them back to the paths of sobriety and virtue. Do they endeavor to effect this, by ceasing to mind high things, and by condescending to men of low estate? No—but instead of going among them, and taking this unhappy class of our fellow creatures by the hand, and leading them by encouragement and persuasion to the paths of temperance and reformation, they have, in substance, said, "stand by thyself, I am holier than thou." They have minded high things, by placing themselves on an elevation above them, and made them out to be worse than murderers, thieves and robbers, by ascribing all the crimes, that are committed, to the use of rum! This has discouraged and exasperated many, and made them feel that reformation would be of no avail to raise them to be the associates of those, who appeared so anxious to reform them. Their language has, in substance, been—you must reform, give us the credit, but must stand where you are in the lower circles of life, obey our exhortations, and look up to us as your benefactors, but you cannot expect to rank with us, because you have no cash to introduce yourselves into our circles. And as all men desire society, they have remained with their companions in iniquity.

For any class of society to take a station above others, and endeavor to force men to abandon the cup by passing votes or enacting by-laws, that no spirits shall be sold them, is but exciting their rage, and causing the intemperate to drink the more out of revenge, and causing those, that are already temperate, to increase the quantity as an act of defiance. It is a fearful precipice on which we stand as a religious community. Estimating a man's standing in society by his immense wealth, or learned profession, rather than by his integrity and virtue, is attended with the most dangerous circumstances, as we have already noticed. Men cannot be reformed by force, nor by declaiming what a low, mean, unworthy, degraded part of the human race they are.

There is too much pride in our world. We ought to bear in mind that death will soon lay our heads equally low in the dust, and "the worms shall cover us!" O the folly of human pretensions to greatness! Let us not mind high things, but condescend to men of low estate. By preachers and people of all denominations obeying the exhortations of our text, mankind would, in a great measure, be restrained from crime, and certainly from being openly intemperate. If then, we sincerely desire to reform them, and to hold a powerful check upon their conduct, and prove ourselves the benefactors of our race, let us begin the work, by adhering most scrupulously to our text, which exhorts us to be of the same mind one towards another, to mind not high things, but to condescend to men of low estate.

It is the duty of preachers, in particular, to be meek and lowly in spirit—to be humble and watch over the moral maladies of mankind—to break down the arrogant distinctions, which the fashions and riches of the world have set up—to esteem men purely for their moral and intellectual worth, independent of the gifts of fortune, and to visit those, who are given to intemperance, and, by gentle persuasive measures, endeavor to lead them to habits of sobriety. And when this is effected, treat them according to that respect, which their virtues merit. God is kind to the evil and to the unthankful, and ought we to be unkind to them? Heaven forbid.

We have now set before you, what we conceive to be the *principal cause* leading to *intemperance, dishonesty, and crime*. True, there may be some exceptions to this, but we are conscious, that it is the conduct of those very men, who are declaiming against *intemperance and crime*, that first drives their fellow creatures into those deplorable haunts of vice. They do this *indirectly*, and perhaps *innocently*. They do it by giving too much reputation and influence to the wealthy class of the community, by paying too much homage and respect to gold, and by withholding, from the virtuous poor, that respect which their conduct merits. We cannot set this truth before you in a more forcible light, than by relating, from memory, an anecdote of Dr. Franklin, with which we will conclude. The rich merchants and professional men in Philadelphia proposed to form themselves into a social circle from which all *mechanics* were to be excluded. The paper, drawn up for the purpose, was presented to Dr. Franklin for his signature. On examining its contents, he remarked that he could not consent to unite his name inasmuch as by excluding mechanics from their circle, they had excluded God Almighty, who was the greatest mechanic in the universe!

SERMON XVII

"And be ye kind one to another, tender hearted, forgiving one another, even as God for Christ's sake hath forgiven you." Ephesians iv. 32.

A tender heart is the kind boon of heaven, and forgiveness is a virtue too little exercised in the common intercourse of life. Men are too apt to be in character Pharisees. They are too apt to love those that love them, and hate their enemies. Retaliation is inconsistent with the spirit of the gospel, and is a vice deeply to be stigmatized and deprecated by all lovers of peace and morality. By retaliation, we are to understand the injuring of another because he has injured us. This spirit of revenge betrays a contracted mind in which the feelings of compassion and forbearance never found a permanent abode. A man of a peevish, irritable and revengeful temperament, is to be pitied, instead of being injured in return. By retaliating the evil he may have done, you involve yourself in the same condition of meanness, and in your turn become the injurer.

All those men, whose names are rendered illustrious and immortal, have been distinguished for a spirit of forbearance, kindness and mercy. Were there no examples of rashness—no failings and imperfections among men, there would, then, be no opportunity to distinguish ourselves by a spirit of forgiveness. God has so constituted the present existence of his creatures, that the perfections of his divine character might be manifested to them in the unchanging exercise of his paternal compassion and forgiveness; and thus afford them an opportunity to imitate himself in the exercise of those exalted feelings, which emanate from heaven.

We are not, however, to understand that tenderness of heart and forgiveness are to be exercised to the utter exclusion of the principles of honor and justice. If our children offend, or our dearest earthly friend do wrong, we are to manifest the feelings of tenderness and forgiveness, but these ought not to induce us to overlook their crimes or faults, by remaining silent in regard to their vices. This would be suffering our compassion to degenerate into weakness. It would in fact be hardness of heart. It would betray a spirit of indifference to their dearest interest, as by our silence, they might remain in blindness to the demerit of their deeds, and hurry on to the ruin of their reputation, and consequently, of their earthly happiness. True tenderness of heart makes us watchful over the conduct of those we love, and with whom we are connected in life— moves us to lay naked before them their faults, so that they may early correct them, and thus inspires their hearts with tenderness, and prompts them to regard the happiness, feelings and welfare of others. It is immaterial how near and dear your friend may be, you should, by the feelings of mercy, be induced to tell him his faults, however much it may wound his heart. The wise man says "the wounds of a friend are faithful; but the kisses of an enemy are deceitful." Too many parents, for want of determination of character, and for suffering their compassion to degenerate into weakness and remaining blind to the faults of their children, having seen them come to some disgraceful end—a state prison, or even the gallows. This, instead of being true tenderness of heart, was infatuation and the worst species of hardness and insensibility to the welfare of their offspring. On the other hand, we ought never to suffer a spirit of revengeful indignation to slumber in our bosoms, ready on every trivial occasion to awake into resentment and retaliation. In fine, we ought to imitate our God in feelings and conduct towards each other, as it is expressed in our text. But many suppose that God is filled with feelings of revengeful indignation towards his creatures, and that the period is rolling on when he will cease to be merciful, and will commence torturing us in the future world for the sins committed in this, and that too, when punishment can do no good to the sufferer—when reformation will be out of his reach. To torment a frail dependent creature, under such circumstances, would be the most degrading species of revenge. And if this is the conduct of God, then we must practice the same, because we are commanded to imitate him. Our text says—"Be yea kind one to another, tender-hearted, forgiving one another; even as God for Christ's sake hath forgiven you."

In this passage, our Father in heaven is held up to the world as the model of *kindness tenderness and forgiveness*, that mortals are to imitate. God is the moral standard to which every bosom ought to aspire. The highest perfection and loveliness of man fall infinitely short of the intrinsic loveliness and divine perfection's of Jehovah.

If he is the standard of moral excellence which we are to imitate, then we must admit that the copy far exceeds the imitation. If man is called upon to act like God in order to improve his character and affections, then God is better than man, and every opposing objection must, forever, fall to the ground. Perhaps it may be said, that all denominations of men allow him to be so. This is not correct. It is true, they *say this* in so many words. But words are one thing, and what a doctrine involves is quite *another*. I might believe, and most rigidly maintain, that an earthly father had prepared a palace of comfort for his five *obedient* children, and a furnace of fire to torture his five *disobedient* children; and suppose he had dealt with his ten children as above stated;—with what propriety could I step before the public, and contend that he was the best man in America? Even were I persuaded, in my own mind, and firmly believed him to be the best man in existence, would either my *belief or acknowledgment* make it a fact? No; every man of common sense, and common humanity would think me deranged. My saying that he was good, and even believing him so, could not alter the awful reality, but would be an evidence of my want of consistency and propriety. He would still be a bad unfeeling man, and in no comparative sense so good as that father, who should punish his children in mercy, and for their future amendment and benefit.

But what is all this compared with the character that thousands ascribe to the God, who rules above? It is no more than the drop to the unmeasured ocean: because those five children would soon cease to suffer; but God, they contend, will torture without mercy or end, millions on millions of his poor dependent creatures for the sins of a short life! The most abandoned, and unrelenting savage, that roams the American forest—the worst wretch in human form would not do this, but release, at length, the sufferer from pain. And those, who contend that God will not release, but on the contrary involve the victim of his ire deeper in who, attribute to him a character infinitely worse, than the most cruel and degraded of our race, and no argument, to the contrary, can be for one moment maintained. If a man desire the holiness and happiness of all his fellow creatures, and would bring them to a glorified state of beatitude in heaven, had he the power, and still contends that God will not, it is elevating his goodness far above the goodness of God. And for any man to come forward with this acknowledgment on his lips, and yet address the benignant Parent of all, and, in prayer, acknowledge him to be the best of all beings, is only using words without propriety or meaning. There is no sense, no reason in such logic. It completely contradicts itself, and what is contradictory cannot be true.

Would you save all men from sin and its attendant misery if you could? O yes, is the answer, I would, and carry them all in the arms of unbounded benevolence to glory. Well, has God the power to do it? Yes, is the reply. But do you believe that he will exert his power so as to accomplish it? No says the objector, I believe that he will sentence a large portion of his erring offspring to endless and inconceivable wo. Very well; then you are the best being of the two. And it is a melancholy circumstance to these unfortunate beings, that you are not on the throne of the universe. If this be so, then our text ought to be reversed. God ought to copy your tenderness, and forgive men as you do! We are certainly called upon to conform our conduct to the best standard, and to imitate the *best* being. If you are the *best*, then God and man ought to be called upon, and *entreated* to imitate you! No; says the objector, God is superlatively the best being in the universe. You may talk, and tell me so, till the morning sun sinks beyond the western hills, and yet your *creed* will contradict every word you utter. What you have just acknowledged, unchangeably stares you in the face. You say, that you would forgive all, save them from sin, and raise them to a blessed eternity, if you had the power. This power, you say, God possesses, and yet you *believe*, and that he will not do it. It is certainly an unfortunate circumstance to the human family, if their Father in heaven is destitute of that goodness which you feel! From whom did you receive all those compassionate feelings of heart? Why says the objector, God gave them to me. But how can God give you what he has not himself? If you possess more benevolence than God, you could not have received it from him; because on this principal he did not have it in possession to give. Surely he could not communicate to you, or any other being, what he did not originally possess. From what source, then, did you derive so much tenderness and love? There must, certainly, be some being in the universe in whose bosom is rooted as much benevolence and love as you feel, or how could it have been communicated to you from another? Now, where did you get it? God gave it to me, says the objector. This cannot be, because your doctrine proves, that you have more love than the God who made you! If you insist that he has given it to you, has he not in such case, given you more than he originally possessed? He has. If so, endless misery may be true; for on this principle he has none left!

The scriptures teach that "God is love"; and all his works speak the same language—saying, "the Lord is good, and his mercies endure forever." But how good is he? The doctrine of endless wrath says, he is not as good as you. You are but a small stream from an infinite ocean of love; and yet this little stream is greater than the ocean from which it issues, and rises far above its fountain head! Can this be true? Impossible. O, do you not perceive how your own feelings, which you daily experience, contradict your creed! You feel, desire, and pray for the salvation of all men, and if you had the power, all your feelings, prayers and desires would be carried into execution. And yet your doctrine denies, that God, the fountain, in which all your affections originate and live, will do it;—and at the same time you say, that you have no love only what he gave you! What inconsistencies, contradictions and blindness are here! Man, a small drop, from the benevolent fountain God, is willing to do, what the source from whence he came is unwilling to do! Then a drop of love, in the human bosom, is more tender and benevolent than an ocean in the God, who placed it there!

We all know, that the fountain must be more extensive than the stream it sends forth—yea, larger, than all its running streams put together. This we know to be correct, as well as we know, that the sun enlightens the world. Let us then collect these little streams into one. Bring, if you please, into one body, the love and benevolence of men and angels, of cherubim and seraphim—stretch your thoughts to unnumbered worlds, extract the love from countless bosoms, and condense the whole into one being. How great, lovely, and adorable, would that creature be! Then, let the question be put to him—from whence did you derive all those noble qualities of love, mercy and goodness? He replies, *from my Father God!* Now, we must grant, that God far exceeds him in goodness, because this noble creature is but an emanation from him—and the good desires of this creature would be equal to the good desires of the countless millions of men and angels in all worlds; and could have no other intentions only those, which goodness and mercy dictate—and goodness itself can do nothing contrary to its own nature, any more than ice can burn or fire freeze. This creature would desire the happiness of all; and yet even he is but a small rivulet flowing from the crystal fountain of life and being! This creature would institute a government *perfectly merciful*; and mercy would, of course, require, that the *disobedient* should be punished to bring them to *obedience*, and perfect them in the same state of glorification and love with that being itself.

"God is *love*," and it, therefore, follows that he is *love* to every creature he has made, and it is utterly impossible that he can do any thing contrary to his own nature. "He cannot deny himself." He will, therefore, do all that love dictates. It is consistent with parental love to punish for the good of its offspring, but not to punish unmercifully. But inquires the objector, does God punish for the good of his creatures? We will let Paul settle this question—Heb. Xii. Chap. "For whom the Lord loveth he chasteneth, and scourgeth every son whom he receiveth. But if ye be without chastisement, whereof *all* are partakers, then are ye bastards and not sons. Furthermore, we have had fathers of our flesh which corrected us, and we gave them reverence; shall we not much rather be in subjection unto the Father of spirits and live? For they verily for a few days chastened us after their own pleasure, but he for our profit that we might be partakers of his holiness. Now no chastening for the present seemeth to be joyous, but grievous; nevertheless afterward it yieldeth the peaceably fruit of righteousness unto them that are exercised thereby." Now show us, if you can, any punishment which God inflicts, that contradicts his paternal goodness. It cannot be done. He has threatened and inflicted *everlasting punishment* upon nations, as such, but not a solitary passage can be produced from Genesis to Revelations, where he has threatened any individual with *everlasting* punishment.

God is the adorable fountain of all tenderness, love, and compassion, and no mother's son was imbued in the fount of mercy like his, who was "the brightness of his glory and the express image of his perfections." True, her yearnings over the babe of her bosom are great; still they bear but little comparison to him who breathed those feelings there. God compares himself to the mother. "Can a woman forget her sucking child"? Woman, being of a more delicate formation than man, possesses a mind susceptible of more fine, deep, and lasting impressions than his. The affections of her soul, when fully roused into action, and fixed upon their object, are deeper than those of man, extend far beyond the compass line of his, and nobly range those sequestered haunts—those delightful fields of mental felicity, where his finest affections never penetrated. Let her heart once become fixed upon its darling object, and it is immaterial in what situation in life we contemplate her—whether prosperous or adverse, we behold the same unshaken constancy, the same bright and burning flame. Her love to her children is pure as the dew-drops of the morning, high as the heavens and unchanging as the sun. It scorns dictation, bids defiance to oppression, and never for one moment loses sight of its object. No disappointments that cross her path, no scenes of adverse fortune that darken her sky, can wrench it from her grasp, obscure it from her vision, or tear assunder the silken cord that binds it to her heart.

The truth of these remarks we see verified in that unwearied watchfulness and care, which she exercises over her children in supplying their countless, and ever varied little wants; in allaying their little griefs, in soothing their tender hearts by the soft whispers of encouragement and love; in hushing them to repose and in watching over the slumbers of their pillow. Are her children exposed to danger, and full in her view? Then no devouring flame, that wraps her dwelling in destruction—no rolling surges that lash the foaming main, can, in such a moment of peril, over-awe her spirit, or deter her from rushing into the very jaws of death to save them. Are they sick? Sleepless she sits beside their bed, and watches every breath they draw. Are they racked with pain? Her soul inhales the pang; and freely drinks at the same fount of agony, and breathes over them the prayer of mercy. Love is that *attribute* in her nature to which all the *others* are subservient. It is the *shrine* at which they all bow, the *centre* to which they all gravitate. If her children do wrong, she freely forgives.

Has God given the mother all these noble affections, and does he feel less to his helpless, sinful and erring children? Let God answer—"Can a woman forget her sucking child, that she should not have compassion on the son of her womb? Yea, they may forget, yet will not I forget thee."

[Concluded in our next.]

SERMON XVIII

"And be ye kind one to another, tender hearted, forgiving one another, even as God for Christ's sake hath forgiven you." Ephesians iv. 32.

In our last, we showed that that compassion, tenderness, and love of our Father in heaven, are the origin of all the sublime affections in the human bosom, and from this acknowledged fact, have shown that he is infinitely more regardful of the welfare of his offspring than the tender mother, with whom he compares himself; is of the welfare of her sucking child. We now resume the subject.

In our text, we are called upon to forgive one another, as God has forgiven us. In examining this point, we are to be guided by what he has revealed. The question here arises, how many does God command us to forgive? He commands us to forgive *all*, even our enemies. This then must be forgiving them as he does. He therefore forgives all. He commands us to bless them that curse us, and to pray for them that despitefully use us, and persecute us, that we may be the children of our Father in heaven. Does God command us to do more than he is willing to do himself? No, he lives up to his own command. If God requires us to forgive, even as he does, and then commands us to love and forgive *all*, then he loves, and forgives *all*, otherwise he would violate his own command; and then there would be no resemblance between his forgiveness and ours. Even as God, for Christ's sake hath forgiven you, so ought ye also to forgive one another.

Would you forgive all, and bring them home to glory? Yes. Will God? No, says the objector, he will not forgive his enemies, but his friends only. Then you must not forgive all. Do you ask why not? Because you are to forgive, *even* as God. He is the standard you are to imitate. If you forgive more than God, you are better than he. He cannot command you to do different from himself. If God requires you to love and forgive *all*, while he himself will forgive only a part, then God acts contrary to his own command. We are exhorted in the text *to be kind, tender-hearted and forgiving even as he is*. Do your kindness, tenderness, and forgiveness extend to all, and desire the happiness of the universe? Yes. Then also does that of God, or else you are, in every sense of the word, better than he. You differ from, instead of imitating God. If so, you are doing wrong, because you are violating the text. He commands you to be kind, tender, and forgiving *only as he is*;—and you contend that his kindness, tenderness and forgiveness, extend to a part only, and that all the rest he will torture world without end.

But, says the objector, God is now kind, tender, forgiving, and merciful to all; but he will not be so, when they enter eternity, for "the doors of mercy will then be shut." How do you know that—who told you so? Will God change in some future day? If he change, he will not be the same being, he is now. I thought, he was the same yesterday, today, and forever, without variableness or even the shadow of turning. I thought he was the same Jehovah in all worlds. Do you intend to make him kind, tender, and forgiving *here*, but unkind, unforgiving, and hard-hearted to a part of his offspring *hereafter?* If you intend to change both the nature and character of the Almighty in the future world, then you and myself are done arguing. That doctrine is, certainly in a pitiful condition, which drives its advocate to the necessity of changing the Almighty wholly into another being to support it. "God so loved the world, even when dead in trespasses and sins," as to deliver up his Son to "taste death for every man." And being unchangeable, he could never hate them. In our text, God commands us to forgive as he has forgiven. How many does God forgive? Ans. As many as he commands you to forgive. How many is that? *All, even your enemies—to bless and curse not.*

We will now introduce the question—If God has not forgiven a man today, will he ever forgive him? I answer no, for he is unchangeable. We are to apt to think that our Creator is altogether such an one as ourselves—that he loves one day, and hates the next—that he is in reality angry one hour, and pleased the next—or that he holds a grudge one moment and forgives the next, if we will only ask him to do so. But all such ideas are calculated for children—for babes in Christ. The scriptures come down to the weakest capacity; but this is no reason we should always continue children, but rise in knowledge to the strength of manhood. We ought not to be "ever learning and never able to come to the knowledge of the truth." Paul said to his brethren "when for the time ye ought to be teachers, ye have need that one teach you" &c. "When I was a child, I spake as a child, I understood as a child, I thought as a child; but when I became a man, I put away childish things."

The Scriptures are calculated for every capacity—for a child as well as a philosopher. We must rise from one degree of glory to another. We are not to fasten our minds down on the inventions of men, and live and die children. No—we must "forget the things that are behind, and reach forward to those that are before." As full grown men, we are not to suppose that prayer of any mortal can move the Almighty to pardon him. But says the objector, if we sincerely ask God to do thus and so, he will certainly grant our request. Very well, admit this for a moment. God, you say, will answer every *sincere* prayer. Now suppose two armies are to meet in battle, one from France and the other from Holland. The hour when the engagement is to commence is precisely one month from tomorrow noon. Every day, there are millions of sincere prayers offered to God to give them the day. Holland, with one voice, prays for victory and for the preservation of her subjects; and France, with united supplication, prays right the contrary. How, we ask, are all those *sincere* opposing petitions to be answered? Impossible. Again—one denomination prays for the prosperity of its cause, and the destruction of error. And as each believes all others to be in error, of course pray for their downfall. If the Lord answered their petitions, all denominations, of course, of course would fall! One man prays for rain, and another, that it may not rain. If God answered all these petitions, he would be as changeable, not as *one man*, but as the whole human family together.

As it respects God's pardoning the human race, I contend that this pardon existed from the beginning. Do not the Scriptures declare that God chose us *in Christ* before the foundation of the world? Yes, for "he calleth those things which be not as though they were." Well, could we be chosen *in Christ* without being pardoned? No, for the apostle says, "he that is *in Christ* is a new creature;" and, certainly, a man cannot be a new creature *in Christ* without being pardoned in the mind of Deity. If then in the omniscient mind of God, to whom there is no future, they were chosen *in Christ* before the foundation of the world, then in his mind, they must also have been pardoned before the world began. God never does a new act. By *pardon* we are not to understand the clearing of a guilty man from deserved punishment, but an entire deliverance from a disposition to sin. The period, when we are to be released from sin, is through death, where the earthly nature, with all its wants and temptations to sin, falls, and the heavenly nature rises in incorruption and glory through a resurrection from the dead. Is not this the day of redemption when we are set free? Yes, so saith the Scripture. Well do not *redemption, remission, and forgiveness* mean the same thing? They do. Then our *pardon, remission* or redemption will be *realized* through death and the resurrection. We will produce the Scriptures "in whom we have *redemption* through his blood, even the *forgiveness* of sins according to the riches of his grace." Here forgiveness and redemption are used synonymous, and are declared to be *through the blood of Christ*—that is, through his death, as a sacrifice for sin. Sin cannot exist beyond the sacrifice designed to take it away. He is represented as taking away the sin of the world under the figure of a *Lamb*. Sin will come to a finish, under the first covenant, exactly where Christ said "it is finished," at which moment the vail, concealing the "holy of holies," will be rent in twain, and the second covenant be opened. If we step beyond what Christ has said, we may as well give up the Scriptures, and trust to our own vain imaginations. There sin will end; and that is *dismission*, pardon or redemption from it. "O death! Where is thy sting? O grave! Where is thy victory? The *sting* of death is *sin*, and the *strength* of sin is the *law*—but thanks be to God, who giveth us the victory, through our Lord Jesus Christ."

Now, here it is represented, that our victory, over *sin and death*, is *when* we rise to immortal glory. Our *victory* over sin is at the *same instant* with our victory over *death*; and who will deny that our *victory over death* will be at the resurrection? The objector may as well deny our victory over *death* at the resurrection, as to deny our *victory over sin* at that period. The whole is said to be "through Christ." He was our "forerunner" and "first fruits" to represent our condition *there*. When he expired, he was free from *pain*, and when he arose, he was free from *temptation*. So when we pass the same scene, we shall be like *him*, who is our "resurrection and life," otherwise the harvest will not be like "the first fruits."

God, then pardoned the human race, *in Christ*, when he made them. How? Ans. By ordering their existence in such a manner, that they should be freed from sin through death and the resurrection. That is the day of our final discharge—the day, when the prisoner shall be set free—the day, when our redemption shall come. But asks the objector, are we not to *realize* our pardon in this world? Ans. Only *through faith* in the *reality*. We look forward, and anchor our hope within the veil of death, and enjoy our pardon, or redemption, only by an eye of faith. This "faith works by love and purifies the heart." It causes us, in a great measure, to break off our sins by righteousness. But this has no influence, whatever, over the sins already committed. For *them*, we must still continue to feel miserable. Punishment is *certain*. From the sins that are committed, we only enjoy our pardon or redemption from them through faith in Christ the resurrection. Paul told the believers, that if there were no resurrection, their faith was vain, they were yet in their sins. This proves that they only enjoyed the pardon of their sins through faith in the resurrection, otherwise I see no force in his language.

But inquires, the reader, why do you pray that God would pardon our sins? Ans. I do not pray to turn the Almighty from his will and purpose; but humbly trust, that I spend my days in searching out what "that perfect will of God is," and then pray in reconciliation to his revealed will. It is wicked to pray what we do not believe. "Whatsoever is not of faith is sin." I believe that God pardoned us from the beginning, and that this pardon will be realized through death and the resurrection. And when I pray that God would pardon our sins, I mean that he would grant us an evidence of that pardon, which unchangeably existed in his eternal mind, by enlightening our understanding in the Scriptures of truth, and giving us correct views of his character as a Being of tenderness and compassion to the children of men. So when we say, God has pardoned us, we do not mean that he has been moved by our petitions to do a new act; but that through the appointed means, he has so far enlightened our minds, that we have received an evidence of that pardon which existed with him from the beginning, and by faith we look forward, believing it will take place through death and the resurrection, as Christ has proved. By this faith we perceive the love of God, and break off our sins by righteousness. But while in the flesh, we feel a thorn—a hell of conscious guilt for the sins we have committed, and though the penitent may beseech

God, that this messenger of satan, buffeting him, may depart from him, yet the answer will be, "my grace is sufficient for thee."

We now perceive how God pardons sin, and yet punishes us for it. The misery, sin brings upon us, is our just punishment, and to be released from it, by the free grace of God, through death and the resurrection, is our pardon and redemption—For example—we say, in a cloudy day, "the sun does not shine;" but still he does. The clouds, just above our heads, prevent his rays from shining upon us. The change is not in the sun. The clouds disperse, and we say, "the sun shines," while in fact he is ever the same. The Scriptures say, "our God is a sun." He is unchangeably the same in all his brilliant perfections. "Sin like a cloud, and transgression like a thick cloud," rise over the mind and darken the understanding. Through this dark medium we look up to God, and think he has changed—that he is angry, and thunders are rolling from his hand, while in fact the whole change is in us. The moment our minds are enlightened by the beams of truth we rejoice, and say God has forgiven us. We receive an evidence of pardon, and enjoy it through faith, while God has remained unchangeably the same.

While we are children in christianity, we speak and act like children; and think if we join together, and pray as loud as we can as though the Lord were "deaf, or all asleep or on a journey," that we can prevail, and make him do as we wish. And while we are children, if we sin, we think the Lord is our enemy, and is angry. Now, this is all well enough for those whose experience has gone no further. We are not to "despise the day of small things," but kindly receive such an one as a babe in Christ, and feed him with milk. But still it does appear to be a pity that thousands, under the gospel, should live and die children.

"Be ye kind one to another, tender-hearted, forgiving one another, even as God for Christ's sake hath forgiven you." Now, we are to forgive as God does. How is that—To hold a grudge one day, and if they ask our pardon, to forgive them the next? No, we must uniformly possess a kind, tender-hearted, forgiving spirit, laying up nought against any one. Forgiveness does not consist in laying up a store of malice and vengeance, till our enemy come, and formally ask our forgiveness. No—he might never come, and then we could never forgive him. We are commanded to love and forgive our enemies whether they ask it, or not. So did our Saviour on the cross, and we are to exercise the same spirit of benevolence and meekness. We must, as our context says—put away all malice, wrath, and evil speaking from among us, and be kind, tender-hearted and forgiving.

Our Father in heaven is the most lovely and adorable of all beings! Under the light of his character, every uncomfortable thought vanishes, and the dawn of a blessed eternity bursts upon us in a flood of glory. By faith we penetrate the veil of immortality, and read our pardon, and justification in letters of blood. Within that veil, we anchor our hope. Faith triumphs over the ruins of death, smiles at the darkness of the tomb, and through Christ within, the hope of glory, bids defiance to the crushing hand of death, and lights up its dreary mansions with the cheering beams of immortal day.

SERMON XIX

"For the time is come that judgment must begin at the house of God; and if it first begin at us, what shall the end be of them that obey not the gospel of God? And if the righteous scarcely be saved, where shall the ungodly and the sinner appear?" 1 Peter iv:17, 18.

Upon this passage, the believers in endless misery lean for the support of that sentiment, and on many occasions it is quoted with an air of triumph as though the passage itself, without comment, were sufficient to silence all objections. Here they have one advantage of Universalists; and of this advantage they do not forget to avail themselves—viz: the prejudices of early education. But we sincerely call their application of this passage in question, and shall stand forth in defense of the triumphs of Jesus Christ over all sin, and pain and death, fully believing that the hand of heaven "shall wipe tears from off all faces." We will attempt to show,—

First—What we are to understand by *judgment* beginning at the house of God.

Second—Who were the *righteous*, and in what sense they were scarcely saved.

Third—Show who were the *ungodly*, and where they appeared.

First—What we are to understand by judgment beginning at the house of God. Jesus Christ chose him twelve disciples and commenced the great work the Father sent him to do. To them he disclosed many events, that God would in a future day bring upon the world. He pointed them forward with more than human accuracy into the approaching revolutions of time, and painted out in noon-day light those astonishing disasters that would one day burst like a thunderclap on the thoughtless nations. He marked their certainty, and warned them accordingly. Among the many things, that lay buried in the vista of future years, was the destruction of Jerusalem. This was a point that most solemnly concerned the disciples of Jesus. It was no less than the destruction of their nation.

Christ was with his disciples in the temple, that splendid edifice which was forty and six years in building, and, in their presence and for the last time, addressed the stubborn Jews. He pointed out the many crimes of which they and their fathers had been guilty in shedding the blood of the prophets, and persecuting those who were sent unto them as the messengers of Jehovah. They had also made void the law of God through their traditions. While pointing out these things, and setting them home like a thunderbolt to their hearts, he pronounced them hypocrites, blind guides, devourers of widows' houses, and declared that all the righteous blood shed upon the earth should be required of of that generation. While rehearsing these things to them, Jesus had a perfect view of all their approaching sufferings. Many of them were to be starved to death. He saw by a prophetic eye the indulgent father and fond mother weeping over their infant train, who were begging for bread, but no way to procure it. Eleven hundred thousand he saw in a state of starvation, who were to fall by famine, sword and pestilence. He saw their cruel enemies surround the walls of their city, who would allow no sustenance to be given them, but determined to reduce them by hunger and sword to one common grave. All these things, that were coming upon them, rushed at once upon the mind of the compassionate Redeemer of the world. The affecting scene moved so strongly upon his heavenly feelings, that he dropped the the melancholy subject and burst into a flood of tears. He beheld the city and wept over it—"O Jerusalem! Jerusalem! Thou that killest the prophets and stonest them which are sent unto thee, how often would I have gathered thy children together, even as a hen gathereth her chickens under her wings, but ye would not!" He then left the temple for the last time; but as he was departing from it, his disciples, astonished at his denunciation, and regretting that such a magnificent edifice should be destroyed, exclaimed—"Master, see what manner of stones and what buildings are here!" And he said unto them "there shall not be left here one stone upon another that shall not be thrown down." The disciples immediately asked him saying, "tell us when shall these things be, and what shall be the sign of thy coming and of the end of the world?" By the end of the *world* we are to understand the end of the Jewish *age*. As they asked him the *signs* portending this terrible destruction, so that they might know when it was nigh at hand, he immediately proceeded to point them out, and warned them to flee to the mountains of Judea for safety.

The signs are as follows—many false Christs should arise, there should be wars and rumors of wars, nation should rise against nation, kingdom against kingdom, and there should be famines, pestilences and earthquakes in diverse places. Then shall they deliver you up to be afflicted, and shall kill you, and ye shall be hated of all nations for my name sake. Then shall there be great tribulation such as was not since the beginning of the world to this time, no nor ever shall be. The most prominent *sign* he gave them, and one that more immediately concerned his disciples, was that they should deliver them up to be afflicted, and they should be brought before kings and governors for his name's sake. "But, (says Jesus) when they persecute you in one city, then flee ye to another."

Christ gave his disciples plainly to understand, that when the Jews began their persecutions against his followers, then the destruction of Jerusalem was nigh at hand. After giving these instructions to his disciples, he laid down his life, and on the third day he arose, triumphing over death and leading captivity captive. His disciples soon after commenced the spread of the gospel of peace, and waived the banners of the cross over kings and subjects, calling upon them to bow to the reign of Jesus Christ, who was King of kings, and

Lord of lords. They proclaimed a religion so contrary to the partial notions of the Jews and the traditions of the Elders, that it began at length to meet with violent opposition. The disciples agreeably to the direction of Jesus fled for safety from city to city, till the tumult and opposition became general. Christianity gathered force and popularity so rapidly, that the Romans, it appears, gave permission to the Jews to imprison and take life. The disciples and christians had now no place of safety to flee to, from the gathering storm of persecution and death. Amidst these disastrous scenes, Peter called to mind the *warnings and signs* his risen Lord had pointed out as a solemn premonition that the destruction of Jerusalem and of their persecutors, was nigh at hand, and in view of the approaching calamity over which Jesus wept, Peter exclaims, "The time is come that judgment must begin at the house of God, and if it begin first at us, what shall the end be of them that obey not the gospel of God?" Thus we, see that what is meant by *judgment* beginning at the *house* of God, is *persecution* beginning at the *christians*, which persecution was a *sign* to them that the destruction of that nation was nigh at hand. The reader will perceive that what the apostle calls "*house of God,*" he afterwards calls "*us*," in the same sentence, and must refer to the christians, who are in many scriptures called the *house, temple, and building* of God. [See Heb. iii:6. Eph. ii:21, 22.] That the persecutions were stated by Christ as a *sign* of the impending judgment of God upon the Jews, is evident from the words of Paul, 2 Thess. i:5, where he calls them "a manifest *token* of the righteous judgment of God" upon the unbelieving Jews, the persecutors of the christians.

Second—Who were the righteous, and in what sense they were scarcely saved. The righteous, mentioned in the 18th verse, mean the same persons called "*the house of God,*" and "*us*," in verse 17th, and has reference to those christians *only*, who lived previous to the destruction of the temple, and not to any christians that lived subsequent to that event, much less does it refer to all the righteous that have ever existed or shall hereafter exist, as common opinion asserts.

Under this head, we were also to show in what sense these righteous were *scarcely* saved. It could not mean that their salvation in the future world was *scarce* or uncertain; for it is *certain* in the counsels of God, and in all things well ordered and *sure*. He has given to his Son the heathen for an inheritance and the uttermost parts of the earth for a possession. And all the Father hath given him shall come unto him, and he will raise them up the last day. He is mighty to save to the uttermost all that come unto God by him; and no one will deny that the righteous come unto him. How then can their eternal salvation be denominated *scarce*? Impossible. How then are the scriptures to be reconciled with our text, when they declare eternal life to be the gift of God—that we are saved by grace—that help is laid upon one mighty to save—that his arm is not shortened that it cannot save; and that the power of God is to be exerted at the resurrection in making them equal unto the angels? The answer is easily given—our text has no reference whatever to the immortal world, to a judgment at the end of time, nor to the final condition of the human family; but simply refers to the narrow escape of the christians from the destruction of Jerusalem, when they fled with their lives in their hands to the mountains of Judea for safety.

In the 24th chapter of Matthew Jesus clearly describes the dreadful scene. He says—"Then let them which be in Judea flee into the mountains. Let him which is on the house top not come down to take any thing out of his house. And woe unto them that are with children and to them that give suck in those days!" [Why? Because they could not remain in the mountains during the period that the city was besieged by the Romans.] "But pray ye that your flight be not in the winter neither on the Sabbath day." [Why? Because in the winter you would perish with cold—and if your flight from the city be on the Sabbath day, the Jews will stone you to death for traveling more than three miles.] "For there shall be great tribulation, such as was not since the beginning of the world to this time, no, nor ever shall be. And except those days should be shortened there should no flesh be saved;" [Saved from what? Ans. From death.] "but for the elect's sake those days shall be shortened." That is, for the sake of the christians who fled to the mountains, God shortened the days of the siege. Let us hear Dr. Adam Clarke, a Methodist Commentator, on this—"Josephus computes the number of those who perished in the siege at eleven hundred thousand, besides those who were slain in other places; and if the Romans had gone on destroying in this manner, the whole nation of the Jews would in a short time have been entirely extirpated [destroy completely, as if down to the roots]; but for the sake of the elect, the Jews, that *they* might not be utterly destroyed, and for the christians particularly, the days were shortened. These partly through the fury of the zealots on the one hand, and the hatred of the Romans on the other; and partly through the difficulty of subsisting in the mountains without houses or provisions, would in all probability, have all been destroyed, either by sword or famine, if the days had not been shortened."

Let us hear Clarke explain how these christians were *scarcely* saved. "But he that shall endure unto the end, the same shall be saved." "It is very remarkable that not a single christian perished in the destruction of Jerusalem, though there were many there when Cestius Gallus invested the city; and had he persevered in the siege, he would soon have rendered himself master of it; but when he unexpectedly and unaccountably raised the siege, the christians took that opportunity to escape." Clarke says "*unto the end*" means "to the destruction of the Jewish polity." Therefore when Peter says, the righteous are *scarcely saved*, he had reference to the dreadful judgment which was coming upon "the wicked and ungodly" inhabitants of Jerusalem for shedding the blood of the righteous, and from this destruction the christians escaped with their lives in their hands to the mountains of Judea for safety as Jesus had directed them. They but just escape— they were *scarcely* saved.

The christians also suffered persecution from the Jews; and Peter draws this inference from it—If we, who obey the gospel of God, have to endure so many persecutions from the Jews—if this judgment begins at us, how much sorer punishment will our enemies have to endure, who obey not the gospel of God? And if we the righteous are scarcely saved from this long-predicted destruction, where will the ungodly and the sinner appear? But how did Peter know that it was at hand? Because the persecutions, which Jesus had given them as a "*sign*" or "*token*" had then commenced at the house of God. The reader will now perceive that Peter was not speaking of a judgment at the end of time, because the judgment of which he was speaking had then commenced—"*The time is come.*" Neither was he speaking of christians generally, nor of salvation in the future world; but of those christians *only* who lived previous to the destruction of the Jewish polity, and of their being saved with *difficulty* by watching the *signs* and fleeing to the mountains of Judea as Jesus had forewarned them.

Luke records the language of Christ more plainly to be comprehended than that of Matthew. "In your patience possess ye your souls. And when ye shall see Jerusalem encompassed with armies, then know that the desolation thereof is nigh. Then let them which be in Judea flee into the mountains, and let them which are in the midst of it depart out," &c. We should be led to suppose that, after the walls of the city were surrounded by an army, it would then have been too late for the christians to save themselves. But Christ as a prophet knew that Cestius Gallus would raise the siege, and fall back to make preparations for a more decisive attack, and thus afford the christians an opportunity to escape. It is evident to every candid reader that Luke expresses in chap. 21st, all that Matthew does in chap 24th and 25th. And that Luke does not refer to a judgment at the end of time is certain from the manner in which he concludes, which is as follows: "And take heed lest at any time your hearts be overcharged with surfeiting and drunkenness, and the cares of this life, and so that day come upon you unawares * * * Watch ye, therefore, and pray always that ye may be accounted worthy to escape all these things that shall come to pass and to stand before the Son of man." Here we perceive that not the least allusion is made to a judgment at the end of time; because there would be no propriety in warning his disciples not to be *drunk or overcharged with the cares of life* at a judgment day thousands of years after their death. The day when the christians were "to stand before the Son of man" was at the destruction of the Jewish polity, and it was to take place in the life time of some of the disciples. Christ says, "there be some standing here that shall not taste of death till they see the Son of man coming in his kingdom." The day of Christ was therefore at hand, and the apostles were warned to keep it in view, and watch the signs that were to precede it. Peter was faithful to these warnings, and when he saw the *signs*, presaging its near approach, he exclaimed—"*The time is come*," &c. This was the day of tribulation, when the christians were scarcely saved from the dreadful fate that overtook their own countrymen, who remained blind till the things that made for their peace as a nation were hidden from their eyes.

[Concluded in our next.]

SERMON XX

"For the time is come that judgment must begin at the house of God; and if it first begin at us, what shall the end be of them that obey not the gospel of God? And if the righteous scarcely be saved, where shall the ungodly and the sinner appear?" 1 Peter iv:17, 18.

In our last we have attended to the first two divisions of our subject—viz: what we were to understand by judgment beginning at the house of God, and who were the righteous, and in what sense they were scarcely saved. We now invite the attention of the reader to the remaining division of the subject. *Third—who were the ungodly, and where they appeared.* By the *ungodly* and the *sinner*, we are to understand the unbelieving Jews, the murderers of Christ and the persecutors of his followers. It has *exclusive* reference to them and not to the ungodly who lived subsequent to the destruction of Jerusalem, much less does it refer to all the wicked that have ever existed, or shall hereafter exist, as common opinion asserts. This needs no further explanation.

Under this head, we were also to show *where the ungodly and the sinner appeared*. We have already had occasion to state, that Peter in our text refers to the destruction coming upon the Jews. The time was come when that judgment of persecution, which began at the christians, was to be returned upon the heads of their persecutors in seven fold vengeance and suffering. Their city and nation were to be destroyed, and their magnificent temple, where their devotions were offered, was to be laid even with the ground. Not one stone was to be left upon another, but the whole become one general heap of ruins. Then according to the prediction of Jesus, was there to "be great tribulation, such as was not since the beginning of the world to this time, no, nor ever shall be." Then was "wrath to come upon them to the uttermost." Then was he to "take vengeance on them that know not God, and obey not the gospel of our Lord Jesus Christ." Then were "the children of the kingdom to be cast out into outer darkness where there was wailing and gnashing of teeth." Then, as a nation, were "they to go away into everlasting punishment;" for "these were the days of vengeance when all things, that were written, might be fulfilled," and "all the righteous blood shed upon the earth, from the blood of Abel to the blood of Zacharias, should come upon that generation."

Titus led the Roman army against them, surrounded the walls of the city on the day of the Passover, where a great part of the Jewish nation were then assembled, and to which others had fled for refuge, being driven by the terror of his arms like chaff before the whirlwind. Here they appeared! Husbands and wives, parents and children, brothers and sisters, (one promiscuous throng) were gazing in breathless solicitude, while consternation and dismay were depicted in every countenance, and fearful expectation pervaded every bosom! Death, a long lingering death, was gathering around them in all its horrors! Old men and young, maidens, matrons and little children poured forth their lamentations to heaven, invoking the protection of the God of Israel. But, alas! "the things, that made for their peace (as Jesus forewarned them) were hidden from their eyes!" Their hour was come, and the triumphant shouts of the enemy were heard around their stubborn walls, which (massy as they were) dropped to the ground under the subduing power of the battering-rams of war. With these massive engines of destruction, they laid the two first walls in ruin! But the third and last wall it was not in the power of the enemy to gain. The Jews fought with desperation, and by valiant exertions kept the enemy at bay, and for a while seemed to triumph in the fond hope of victory over the foe. The Roman army was driven to great extremity, and even to hesitation, while many of their most valiant men fell in action, and impending victory seemed to hang doubtful. In this moment of suspense, they came to a determination to make no further attack upon the city, but guard it and reduce its inhabitants to submission by famine. All supplies were accordingly cut off, and every avenue blocked up by the vigilant Romans. In addition to this, intestine divisions, civil wars and pestilence raged within the walls of the city. Having no employment in fighting the enemy, they fell to butchering each other. These things proved their ruin, and their national sun went down in blood. Every day thousands closed their eyes in death through famine and pestilence; and thousands by endeavoring to escape to the enemy and surrender themselves up as prisoners for safety and protection, were either cut down by the Roman sword, or met the same fate from their own countrymen. Here they appeared! All hopes of life cut off, nothing presented itself to their view, to end their woes, but the certain prospect of an untimely tomb! Fathers, mothers, brothers, sisters, gazing upon each other in silent expectation, saw death gradually advancing in all its horrors. They were driven to the most dreadful extremities, until (is Josephus informs us) "they devoured whatever came in their way; mice, rats, serpents, lizards, even to the spider"—and lastly mothers were driven to eat the flesh of their own children! Here were lamentation and wo indeed! Such tribulation as our Saviour says never was, and never will be. In imagination the mind runs back to the period, and to the fatal spot. It surveys the painful scene, characterized by nought but moral and physical woes—madness and revenge, cruelty and carnage, pestilence and famine, and all the mingled horrors of war! It surveys the starving child clinging to the maternal bosom for help and protection, but alas! That bosom becomes its grave. Here the ungodly and the sinner appeared in deep despair! Unfeeling mortal, do you say that their punishment and sufferings were not sufficiently great, without adding that of immortal pain in the future world? Are you not satisfied without arguing that they ought to suffer endless misery in addition to their woes? Look with an unjaundiced eye over this scene of distress; and as you gaze let justice (if not compassion) once more take the throne of the heart, and then pronounce the shocking sentence of your creed if you can.

That their sufferings were overwhelming is evident from scripture as well as from history. In Lam. iv. The prophet Jeremiah says—"The hands of the pitiful women have sodden their own children, they were their meat in the destruction of the daughter of my people." In Lev. Xxvi. Moses describes their sufferings as follows—"And I will bring a sword upon you, that shall avenge the quarrel of my covenant: and when ye are gathered together within your cities, I will send the pestilence among you, that shall make you few in number; and ye shall be delivered into the hand of the enemy. And when I have broken the staff of your bread ten women shall bake your bread in one oven, and they shall deliver you your bread again by weight; and ye shall eat and not be satisfied. And if ye will not for all this hearken unto me but walk contrary unto me; then I will walk contrary unto you also in fury; and I, even I, will chastise you seven times for your sins. And ye shall eat the flesh of your sons, and the flesh of your daughters shall ye eat." This did come upon the sinner and the ungodly, and it was "according to their sins." Moses, Jeremiah, and Jesus spake particularly of the sufferings of the Jews in the destruction of their city and they all agree in concluding their chapters. Moses in conclusion says, "and they shall accept of the punishment of their iniquities, even because they despised my judgments, and because their soul abhorred my statutes; and yet for all that I will not cast them away neither will I abhor them to destroy them utterly and to break my covenant with them, for I am the Lord their God." And Jeremiah, after describing their sufferings in the 4th chapter of Lamentations concludes with these words—"The punishment of thine iniquity is accomplished, O daughter of Zion," &c. And Jesus, after denouncing upon them the judgments of heaven in Matt. xxiii. Concludes thus: "For I say unto you, ye shall not see me henceforth, till ye shall say, blessed is he that cometh in the name of the Lord." Thus we see that they agree in testifying to the same fact, that the punishment of the ungodly and the sinner, which mean, no other than the Jewish nation in their overthrow and dispersion as we have already noticed, shall end.

I see therefore no arguments, that can be drawn from our text, to prove a future judgment or endless misery in the immortal world. If the objector can see a shadow of evidence in this passage to support such a sentiment, yet I must frankly acknowledge that, for myself, I cannot. There is certainly no word in the text, that has the most distant allusion to the final condition of man. The *judgment* began at the apostles and christians. But is the *"last judgment"* to begin at them? Certainly not. But admit that it is; we would further inquire, did the last judgment begin as early as the days of Peter? Impossible. Then he could certainly not have had any allusion to such a day, for he exclaims: "*the time is come* that judgment must begin at the house of

God." Here the judgment to which he refers had commenced, or at least the *signs* portending it had commenced, and it was to end upon the ungodly inhabitants of Jerusalem. This fact is evident from the context—"Beloved, think it not strange concerning the *fiery trial* which is to try you, as though some strange thing had happened unto you; but rejoice, inasmuch as ye are partakers of Christ's sufferings, that when his glory shall be revealed ye may be glad also with exceeding joy." From this quotation there can arise no misapprehension as to Peter's application of the text, nor of the persons it involves. They were the persecutors of the christians, and no one will dispute that these were the Jews.

If then this judgment was at hand, it cannot of course refer to a period at the end of time; and it is in this case equally certain, that the *scarce salvation* of the christians can have no reference to the immortal world. These facts being irresistible, the argument must be wholly given up that "the ungodly and the sinner" were to appear in a state of inconceivable torment beyond the grave, because the *condition* of "the ungodly" stands in contrast with the *scarce salvation* of the righteous, and this *salvation or deliverance* was to be in a day nigh at hand, and from a tribulation or judgment in which their adversaries and persecutors were to be involved, and the *signs*, by which the apostle was admonished of its proximity, had already appeared when he wrote the words of our text. The meaning of his words, I humbly conceive, is simply this—The time *is come* when the persecutions, predicted by Christ as a *sign* of the approaching destruction of Jerusalem, must begin at us. And if we the righteous who are innocent, have to endure so many "fiery trials," what will the dreadful punishment be of our disobedient persecutors? And if we are *scarcely saved* from this impending destruction, by fleeing to the mountains of Judea, where will our thoughtless and sinful appear? We have endeavored to show you where they appeared—have pointed out the narrow escape of the christians, who were "scarcely saved," and referred you to the *signs* by which Peter knew this judgment was at hand. It is therefore unnecessary to offer any thing further in defense of our views, as the text is, no doubt, plainly understood by every reader.

We close this discourse by noticing one very common objection, made by our religious opposers, to our application of several scriptures. I do this, because I am not aware that it has been done by any Universalist as a *designed* answer to the objection. The substance of the objection is this:—

There is not a passage in the New Testament which speaks of a day of judgment, of the end of the world and of the coming of Christ, but what Universalists apply to the destruction of Jerusalem. Then, they contend, "every man was rewarded according to his works," consequently all subsequent nations are not to be rewarded, nor are they to experience a day of judgment.

In reply to this objection I would remark, that we are not answerable for the many passages which the Saviour and his apostles applied to that event. But if we make a wrong application of any scripture, why do not our opposers point out the error? We will now show why the apostles wrote so much in reference to that period. They do not so frequently speak of that event merely on account of the destruction of their temple city and nation, (though that might justify their frequent reference to it) but there were circumstances of a more imposing and momentous character to attract their attention to that catastrophe. These were the abrogation of the Mosaic rituals and the introduction of a new order of things by Jesus Christ of whom Moses and the prophets wrote. This was a period when every christian was to be delivered from the persecution of the Jews, and the spread of the gospel was to be retarded no longer by their opposition. The Jews as a nation were to be punished for their deeds of blood, and that *spiritual reign or judgment* commence which should pass upon all subsequent generations of men, rewarding every man according to his works.

The *gospel reign* is called "the *judgment of the world*" by Jesus Christ, in the same sense that Moses judged the world two thousand years by the law. Jesus says, "Think not that I will accuse you to the Father, for there is one that *judgeth* you even Moses in whom ye trust." From this it is evident that Moses was then judging the Jews. But this covenant was abolished at the destruction of Jerusalem. Paul says, "he taketh away the *first* that he may establish the *second*." The word of God, in this covenant, is spiritual and sharper than any two-edged sword—it is a discerner of the thoughts and intents of the heart, while that of Moses was outward, and took cognizance of the conduct only. The objections of our opposers are therefore unsound. And though we apply those passages, which speak of a judgment, to the destruction of the Jews, yet that judgment or reign of Christ which then commenced, is yet going on, and will continue till all are subdued to himself. He then came in his kingdom, and will continue to reward every man according to his deeds till his kingdom ends. So we this day experience the effects of his coming, and of his judgment or reign, and are justified or condemned according as we embrace or reject the words of everlasting life. We see therefore the propriety of the apostles dwelling so much upon that great event, which should witness the passing away of the types and shadows and the establishment of the gospel of Jesus Christ.

SERMON XXI

"For as in Adam all die, even so in Christ shall all be made alive." 1 Cor. xv:20.

The death and resurrection of all mankind are a theme of no ordinary moment, and have given birth to many theories and speculations among the advocates of Christianity. The common opinion is that one portion of our race will be raised to immortal life and glory in the future world, and the other to immortal damnation and dishonor—that at the same instant the living will be changed and that the whole human family will, in this condition, be arraigned before the "Judge of quick and dead," and receive their irrevocable sentence for endless joy or endless wo. Others believe, in opposition to these limited views of the divine character, that the resurrection is the closing scene of the great plan of salvation, and that no judgment is to succeed it. This resurrection, they believe, will introduce the numerous posterity of Adam into the same condition of immortal glory and honor, being made, by the power of God, "equal unto the angels, and be the children of God being the children of the resurrection." As to the *judgment day*, they do not believe, that the whole human family will be congregated in one amazing throng at one period of time, but that the judgment of the world, by Jesus Christ, commenced at the destruction of Jerusalem, when the Mosaic dispensation, with all its imposing rituals, passed away, and that this *judgment*, or in other words, this *gospel reign* of Christ, is still progressing, and will completely terminate before the resurrection takes place. Notwithstanding this view of the day of judgment, yet they suppose that the *resurrection day* is a designated period when the cerement of the dead shall burst, and all the slumbering nations, simultaneously, start up from their beds of clay, the living at the same instant be changed to immortal beings, and this countless throng, in one unbroken strain, shout—"O death! Where is thy sting? O grave! Where is thy victory"?

Though this scene would be full, and immortally sublime, and disclose a grandeur which a seraph's eloquence never can describe, yet I take the liberty to dissent from this long and fondly cherished opinion, and will humbly endeavor to present you my views on the immortal resurrection of the human dead. The ideas I have advanced in my sermons on the *new birth*, require me to do this. And no one has more occasion to rejoice than myself, that we are bound by no creeds, and that the preachers of our order encourage and cherish free investigation. Among such able and benevolent theologians, I feel conscious, if I err, that they will endeavor, in the spirit of meekness, to set me right. I therefore hold no one responsible for the ideas I am now about to advance. I am by no means in favor of new theories built upon mere human speculations, nor do I deem it an enviable task to make innovations on the long and universally established opinions of the christian community. I shall simply appeal to the scriptures to sustain me in my present exposition, and by that standard I am willing my views should be tried, for by that alone, they must ultimately stand or fall.

From the text we have selected, it might, perhaps, be expected, that we should proceed to prove the final holiness and happiness of the human family by showing, that he who is "made alive in Christ is a new creature"; but as this has, heretofore been done so often and so ably, we shall confine our attention, principally, to the different scripture accounts of the resurrection of the dead, and endeavor to ascertain whether it is indeed, to take place at the end of time and be general, or whether it is continually transpiring as gradual as the successive deaths of our race in Adam.

And here I would distinctly remark, that the dead are represented as being raised at the coming of Christ. This is admitted and believed by all. But where, I ask, is there in the Book of God *one passage* to prove any coming of Christ after the destruction of the Jewish polity when he commenced his *gospel reign*, called the *judgment of the world?* This was his *second* coming; but where but where is there a *scrap* of scripture to prove his *third* coming at the end of time? For one, I have searched in vain for such testimony. That Christ came in his kingdom, during the life time of the persons he addressed, and then commenced the judgment of the world, is certain. This is not, however, admitted to be that coming of Christ when the dead will be raised immortal. Where then is revealed that *third* coming of our Lord, at the end of time, to raise the dead? I think it will be an unsuccessful task for any man to search it out and bring it forward.

I would not be understood to say, that no destruction will attend this earth. On the contrary philosophy seems to warrant the idea. But the scriptures no not, in my apprehension, reveal such a catastrophe, nor a *third* coming of Christ, nor a general resurrection at that period. The reader may, perhaps, here inquire whether the scriptures do not clearly describe the resurrection of all mankind to be at one instant of time? I answer, no more than they describe the judgment of all mankind to be at the same instant. But, says the reader, the resurrection is to be at the coming of Christ, which must be at some designated period. Very well; the judgment was to be at the coming of Christ to the destruction of the Jewish state, and does not this designate some particular period? If so, how are we judged in the present day? If the judgment day, which *then* commenced, has not yet ended, why may not the resurrection day be still progressing? If you contend, that the dead were all to rise at once, then by the same mode of scripture interpretation, I can prove that all the living were to be judged at once. Acts xvii. 31. "Because he hath appointed A DAY in the which, he will judge the world in righteousness by that man whom he hath ordained, whereof he hath given this assurance unto all men, in that he hath raised him from the dead." 2 Cor. v.10. "For we must all appear before the judgment seat of Christ, that every one may receive the things in body, according to that he hath done, whether good or bad."

Though this event is represented as transpiring in *one day*, and as though all men were literally arraigned at the same instant, still all Universalist admit, that it commenced at the destruction of Jerusalem, has passed upon succeeding generations, and will continue from the present down to subsequent ages, so long as human beings shall have a habitation on earth. This is called the *last day*. Jesus says—"the word that I have spoken, the same shall judge him in the *last day*." So I contend, that though the resurrection is also called the last day, and represented as raising all mankind at one instant of time, still simply means, that the doctrine of Christ (viz. The judgment and resurrection) should, at his coming in his kingdom, be fully revealed to the living by their seeing his prophesies fulfilled in the abrogation of the ceremonial law, and this doctrine of life and immortality be permanently established and commence its sway over the living, as the last and best system of God to man, and this *resurrection day* continue down to all subsequent generations of slumbering dead, raising every man in incorruption and glory. The judgment and resurrection of the world are therefore both progressing, for these two constitute the gospel reign of Christ. He is "the resurrection and life of the world," as well as "judge of quick and dead." Both are to be accomplished in the *last day*, and that day is now progressing. A *general* resurrection, at the last vibrating pendulum of time, cannot I humbly conceive, be substantiated by the oracles of truth, any more than a *general* judgment. I am rather inclined to think that *the judgment of the world by Jesus Christ expresses the whole, including the resurrection and all; even as the high priest, clothed with the breastplate of judgment on the day of atonement, closed his services by raising the nation into the holy of holies, "which was a pattern of things in the heavens."*

If the Scriptures afford us any evidence of the *third* coming of Christ, to raise the dead, for one, I must acknowledge my utter ignorance of the fact. In John (chap. vi.) Jesus several times uses the expression, "and I will raise him up at the last day." If others contend that this has reference to "*the last day of the last generation of the human race on the earth*," yet I must candidly acknowledge, that I cannot see a shadow of evidence to prove this position. The *last day* in this instance, refers to the gospel dispensation, which commenced at the destruction of the temple, and involves the whole reign of Christ. It is synonymous with the "day of Christ" and the "day of the Lord" mentioned in several places by the apostles. Nor do I conceive it means, that Christ would raise them up by his own immediate power, but that God would raise the dead according to that doctrine, which he sent his Son to reveal to men, and this would be fully established in the world, and be believed and felt by Jew and Gentile Christians at the coming of Christ in his kingdom, at the end of that dispensation. *Then* and not till *then* were the predictions of Christ fulfilled, and then were those Christians, who had not seen Jesus after his resurrection, "made perfect in faith."

The dead are to be raised at the *last* trump; by which I understand the *seventh*, for no other *last* is revealed. This trump is mentioned by our Saviour (Matt. xxiv. 31.) and is the gospel trump which was to commence its sound at the destruction of Jerusalem. In Rev. chap. viii, seven trumpets were given to seven angels, who are represented as sounding them in succession, and increasing woes following, till the sixth trumpet sounded. But when the seventh angel sounded and the last dreadful wo passed away, a very different order of things followed. Rev. x. 7. "But in the days of the voice of the seventh angel when he shall begin to sound, the mystery of God should be finished as he hath declared to his servants the prophets." Rev. xi. 15. "And the seventh angel sounded, and there were great voices in heaven, saying, the kingdoms of this world are become the kingdoms of our Lord and of his Christ, and he shall reign forever and ever." Now compare these woes and this subsequent order of things with the tribulations Christ described in Matt xxiv chap. And the subsequent life the righteous entered into, and you will readily perceive that both refer to the destruction of Jerusalem and the commencement of Christ's auspicious reign. (The Revelations were certainly written before that event.) When the seventh angel sounded, Christ came in his kingdom and began his reign; and that he began his reign when the trumpet sounded, and the woes recorded in Matt. Xxiv. And xxv. Chapters took place, will not be denied. This settles the point that the *seventh or last* trump was not to sound at the close of Christ's reign, but at its commencement. And under this last sounding trump the dead were to be raised immortal, and those who were alive when it commenced its sound, were to be suddenly changed in their circumstances and feelings as described in the context. It was the day of their redemption from all their trials and persecutions, and doubts and fears.

That this was the period when the Christians entered the *resurrection day* as well as the *judgment day* under Christ is certain. They entered into the full enjoyment of that most sublime of all doctrines in the faith of which they not only saw the dead raised immortal and free from pain, but felt themselves new beings. They were exalted from the dust to high and "heavenly places in Christ," were "caught up to meet the Lord in the air," were seated "on thrones and made priests and kings to God and reigned with Christ." There "they shone like the brightness of the firmament and the stars forever and ever," recognized the goodness of God in redeeming love, and sang the song of *certain victory* over death and Hades. Then "the kingdom and dominion and the greatness of the kingdom under the whole heaven was given to the saints of the MOST HIGH," and in this "kingdom of their Father they shone forth like the sun." The above promiscuous quotations from Scripture justify the expression, that the living were "changed in a moment at the last trump," which announced to the world the immortal resurrection of the dead. That this trump, whose sound proclaims the resurrection of all mankind, is the gospel trump, the doctrine of Christ, we cannot doubt.

That the change of the living, in the context, has any reference to changing them into immortal beings, I cannot admit without further evidence. It is contrary to the whole tenor of revelation—it is contrary to our text, which declares that all, who are made alive in Christ first die in Adam. As the change of the living is an important point in our present investigation, we will give it further attention. That the Christians were to experience a great and sudden change at the destruction of Jerusalem is certain. They were to be delivered from all their trials and persecutions, and be raised into the full and felicitous enjoyment of the reign of Christ. Those Christians, who had not seen our Saviour alive from the dead, who had believed on the testimony of his apostles and of the "five hundred brethren," were delivered from all their doubts and fears on seeing his predictions fulfilled, were perfected in faith, and their "hearts established unblamable in holiness." This was to them a resurrection day, not only in reviving their faith and hope in the doctrine of the immortal resurrection of all that died in Adam, but in delivering them from their sufferings, and raising them into the sublime enjoyments of the reign of Christ. In reference to this period, Jesus says, "thou shalt be recompensed at the resurrection of the just." And Paul says, "If by any means I might attain unto the resurrection of the dead, not as though I had already attained, either were already perfect." What sense would there be in his saying—if by any means I might, by my exertions, become an immortal being, not as though I had already attained to immortal existence? No sense at all. But the apostles meaning is clear, if we render it thus—If by any means I might continue faithful unto the end, and obtain a crown of life in the first resurrection at that day when Christ shall come in his kingdom to destroy his enemies and to deliver and elevate Christians to honor. We shall notice this more particularly in our next when we come to comment on Philippians iii. Chap. Again he says—"Who concerning the truth have erred, saying the resurrection is past already, and overthrow the faith of some." That is, to make the Christians believe that their promised deliverance was past, while they were yet in the midst of their sufferings, was calculated to overthrow their faith. We will notice the change of the living still further. Jesus says, that those, who were in their graves, and had done good, should come forth to the resurrection of life. And Daniel says, that many of them who sleep in the dust of the earth should awake to everlasting life, and those, who were wise, should shine as the brightness of the firmament, and they that turned many to righteousness as the stars forever and ever. Here Daniel and Jesus represent the low, suffering, and distressed condition of the Christians previous to the destruction of Jerusalem, and their final deliverance and exaltation at that period, by sleeping in the dust, being dead in their graves, and suddenly coming forth to life and shining like the brightness of the firmament and the stars forever and ever. This is equivalent with being "caught up in the clouds to meet the Lord in the air."

The above changes are as great and as in instantaneous, as the apostle represents in the context,—"We shall all be changed in a moment, in the twinkling of an eye at the last trump; for the trumpet shall sound and the dead shall be raised incorruptible and we shall be changed." As if he had said we shall suddenly enter into the full fruition of that glorious gospel kingdom, whose trump shall then begin, and continue to sound down to the remotest periods of that "*last day*" proclaiming the incorruptible resurrection of all the dead, and at the same time changing the living from the low, sorrowful, and groveling thoughts of earth to the sublime and joyful contemplations of "life and immortality brought to light through the gospel." So the *last day*, in which the last trump sounds, and the dead are raised, embraces the whole gospel reign of Christ. The *resurrection* is coeval in duration with the *judgment* of the world; for both are called the last day, and both are represented as involving all mankind in one assemblage to be judged and in one assemblage to be raised.

[To be continued.]

SERMON XXII

"For as in Adam all die, even so in Christ shall all be made alive." 1 Cor. xv:20.

We have already shown that the *judgment* of the world is called the "*last day*," in which all human beings are to stand at the Judgment Seat of Christ, and receive according to their deeds. We have shown, that this day commenced at the end of the Jewish age, and is to continue down to all succeeding generations, so long as human beings shall have a habitation on earth. We have shown that the *resurrection* is also called the "*last day*," in which all the dead are to be raised immortal. We have shown that, as a doctrine of God, it was permanently established in the world at the end of the Jewish dispensation—that the last or gospel trump then commenced its sound, proclaiming the immortal resurrection of all who "die in Adam," and at the same time changed those who were then alive—and that it shall continue to sound to the remotest periods of this last day, proclaiming the resurrection of the dead and changing or reforming the living. We have shown that the *judgment and resurrection* constitute the gospel doctrine of Christ, and, as such, both were established in the world at the same time, and are both called the "*last day*," in which all men are in succession to be judged, and raised immortal. The apostle Paul, when discussing to his hearers, either the judgment or the resurrection, looked forward to that interesting period, when they were to be established in the world, and, with a giant effort, grasped in one view, the beginning and end of this brilliant, sublime, and everlasting DAY, and presented it in mental vision to his persecuted and almost desponding brethren as one instantaneous, transporting and triumphant event, in which the world was to be judged, the living changed, the dead raised immortal and incorruptible, and the rapturous song of final victory was to be sung over death, its sting and the grave.

We will now proceed to notice those passages, which are applied to the immortal and general resurrection of the dead, point out their misapplication, and reconcile them with the views we have advanced. We will *first* notice our context. And here it will be necessary to ascertain the condition of those whom Paul addresses. He introduces the chapter by referring to the many witnesses of Christ's resurrection, and commences his argument in proof of this fact, and against those christians, who had not been eye-witnesses, but who had professed faith in his resurrection *merely* on the testimony of the apostles. These christians were suffering persecution, and were, of all men most "miserable" if Christ were not risen from the dead; as in such case, their future deliverance and exaltation at his predicted coming, were but a visionary dream. And as their Lord seemed to delay his coming, "some among them (being discouraged) began to say, there was no resurrection of the dead." The great evidence, to which they were looking for the final proof of his being the true Messiah was the fulfillment of all which the prophets had written of "the daily sacrifice being taken away, the holy people being scattered" and of the glory of the Messiah's kingdom and reign, and of all, which Jesus himself had predicted of his coming to destroy their persecutors, to put an end to the Mosaic dispensation, and to raise them to a state of exaltation in his kingdom. They had not seen Jesus alive from the dead as had the apostles; and however much they might be inclined to credit their testimony, yet their severe persecutions and sufferings, and the protracted period of his coming would, very naturally, create, in their hearts many doubts and fears as to its truth.

These are the persons, whom Paul addresses in our context, and labors to keep them in the faith by presenting the *whole weight* of testimony in favor of the resurrection of Christ, on which he hinged the resurrection of man. He summons before them more than five hundred eye-witnesses, of whom himself was one, to satisfy them of the fact, and summons all the powers of philosophy in nature. He refers them to grain sown in the earth, and its coming forth in a new body. He refers them to all the various species of flesh, of men, beasts and birds on the earth, and to the glory of the sun, moon and stars in the heavens —all differing from one another—to prove that God is able to prepare an immortal body, differing from all these, and raise man immortal! As he passes on, reveling in the greatness of his strength, and absorbed in the immensity of his theme, his argument gathers force, till earth and heaven appear to be in motion before him! He ranges the universe, summons to his aid the power of God, lays his masterly hand upon every fact, gathers them in his grasp, condenses them before his hearers, and, in one overwhelming burst of eloquence, makes the whole bear upon the resurrection of Christ and of man! He refers them to the coming of his Lord, at which time will be the end of the Jewish age. Then their sufferings and persecutions terminate, their darkness, fears and doubts will be removed, they will be ushered into the glorious reign of Christ, behold this *last* and brightest day, hear the *last* joyful trump sounding, see the dead by an eye of faith arising, and themselves as living men changed. These would be Christ's at his coming. Then he would receive his kingdom and begin his auspicious reign.

No fact is more certain than that Christ was to commence his reign at the sound of the *last trump*. Not an instance can be produced, where Jesus has revealed to his apostles, that any trump was to sound subsequent to the one, which announced his coming in his kingdom at the end of the Jewish age. If any one can produce scripture authority where a trump is to sound at the close of his reign, or at the end of time, or even produce testimony to prove the end of time, I will publicly and gratefully acknowledge the favor. Perhaps the 24th verse of the context will be brought forward for this purpose: "Then cometh the end, when he shall have delivered up the kingdom to God, even the Father; when he shall have put down all rule, and all authority, and power." This, as it reads, is no objection to my views; but I contend that this is not a correct rendering of the passage. Every careful reader will perceive, that it stands in perfect contradiction with verse 28th: "And when (notice the word when) all things shall be subdued unto him, then shall the Son himself also be subject unto him that put all things under him, that God may be all in all." This verse teaches a future reign and future subjection, after the kingdom is delivered up to God. What propriety is there in saying, "*when all things are subdued unto him,*" after he has resigned his kingdom? What has he to subdue, after the kingdom is delivered "up to God, even the Father". Certainly nothing. I readily grant, that in the modern edition of the Greek Testament I have before me, it is rendered in the dative case, "*teen basileian to Theo kai Patri;*" "*the kingdom to God even the Father.*" But I perused, several years since, a short criticism by an English writer (whose name I cannot recall, nor the periodical which contained it) on this very phrase in which the author stated that in an early Greek manuscript, he had in his possession, it was rendered in the nominative case, "*teen basileian ho Theos kai Pater.*" This would reverse the present translation, and cause it to read—"*Then cometh the end when God even the Father shall deliver to him (Christ) the kingdom.*" The writer however argued, that as the chapter referred to the general resurrection at the end of time, it seemed to read far better as Christ's mediatoriol kingdom would then terminate. This is mere assertion founded upon preconceived opinions.

I will, however, produce direct authority to support my views. I will here present the reader with Wakefield's translation of this passage, whose scholarship will be doubted by none:

"*Then will the end be, when God the Father delivereth up the kingdom to him, during which he will destroy all dominion, and all authority and power; for he will reign till he hath put every enemy under his feet; and so the enemy death will be destroyed at last.*"

Here, then, we perceive that instead of its referring to the end of time, and to the Son's delivering up the kingdom to the Father, it simply refers to the end of the Jewish dispensation, when the Father delivered to his Son a kingdom, and when he *commenced* his reign. This gives harmony, strength and consistency, to the whole connection closing with the 28th verse, and is in perfect agreement with the whole tenor of revelation, which no where speaks of the end of time. But according to the received translation, he first delivers up the kingdom to God, then commences his reign, subdues all things, destroys death, and is then subject to the Father! Let it be distinctly noticed that this "*end*" is at Christ's coming. But where, I again ask, is revealed a *third* coming of our Saviour?

But again—The Ethiopic version also supports this rendering of the above passage, in agreement with Wakefield, which I consider as sufficient authority to settle the question, at least in my own mind. But even were there no other authority, than the general tenor of revelation, I should feel justified in my present exposition. To contend for a *general* resurrection, we are in the same predicament with the orthodox in contending for a *general* judgment.

The above harmonizes (in my apprehension) with every other part of divine revelation, which embraces the testimony of the prophets, and of Jesus Christ and his apostles, who all speak of the *end* as referring *exclusively* to the termination of the Jewish age, at which time he should come in his kingdom and commence his reign. They also speak of the glory which should follow, and of the success that should attend it. But not *an instance can be produced, where they speak of the end of time.* He is to destroy the last enemy *death*; and this work is effected progressively in this *last day*, as individuals are in *succession* raised from death, and established in their final and blissful condition affording us no revelation when this order of things will terminate. If it is a fact, that God the Father, at the sound of the "last trump," delivered to his Son the kingdom—if this be the correct rendering of the passage, as the whole tenor of revelation seems to justify, then it was at the commencement of his reign; and our views of the *resurrection day* are irresistible. The apostle grasps, in mental vision, the whole subject, and represents it as one great and interesting event, big with sentiments of light and life, in the same sense that he does the judgment of the world, which revolved in his capacious soul as but one single day. The sudden and interesting change he represents as taking place in the living, has reference to the unexpected manner in which this sublime scene would burst on the world. In this he but follows the example of his Lord, who declared he would come as a "thief in the night"—that he would "come quickly," and in an hour they were not aware, and exhorted his disciples to watch.

We will notice one more passage in the context, which may be urged as an objection. "Behold I show you a *mystery*; we shall not all sleep, but we shall all be changed in a moment, in the twinkling of an eye at the last trump; for the trumpet shall sound and the dead shall be raised incorruptible and we shall be changed." The *mystery*, here mentioned, refers to the change of those, who should be found alive at the coming of Christ in his kingdom, produced by the full revelation and establishment of that doctrine, which proclaims the immortal resurrection of all mankind *by being made alive in Christ*. It is the fulfillment of the following scriptures—Eph. i 9,10—"Having made known unto us the *mystery of his will*—that in the dispensation of the fullness of times he might gather together in one *all things in Christ*, both which are in heaven and which are on earth, even in him." This mystery was *then finished* in the full revelation of his will to the doubting christians, whom Paul addresses in the context. This is evident from Rev. x:7—"But in the days of the voice of the *seventh angel* when he *shall begin to sound*, the *mystery* of God *should be finished*, as he hath declared to his servants the prophets." And that he began his reign when the mystery was finished is certain from Rev. xi. 15—And the seventh angel sounded; and there were great voices in heaven saying the kingdoms of this world are become the kingdoms of our Lord and his Christ, "and he shall reign forever and ever." Here we perceive that this *mystery of God's will* was to be finished at the sound of the *seventh or last* trump, which will is, to gather or make alive all things in Christ. And at this time he was to receive his kingdom and reign forever and ever. *"We shall not all sleep, but we shall all be changed,"* has reference to those persecuted christians, who were not to "taste of death till they saw the Son of man coming in his kingdom."

Phil. iii:20, 21—"For our conversation is in heaven, from whence we look for the Saviour, the Lord Jesus Christ; who shall change our vile body, that it may be fashioned like unto his glorious body according to the working whereby he is able even to subdue all things unto himself." That this passage has reference to changing our *natural into immortal bodies* at the resurrection, I see not a shadow of evidence to prove, either in established in their final and blissful condition the passage itself, nor in the context. The context we have already noticed by pointing out the resurrection to which Paul desired to attain. Chap. i:6—"He, that hath begun a good work in you, will perform it until *the day of Jesus Christ."* Chap. iv:5—"Let your moderation be known unto all men. *The Lord is at hand."* "The day of Jesus Christ" and "the Lord is at hand" refer to his coming at the end of the Jewish age, and not to a resurrection at the end of time. Paul gave the Philippians notice of no other coming of Christ. The passage has reference to the change the living were to experience, at this coming of our Lord in his kingdom, by being delivered from their persecutions, doubts and fears, perfected in faith, and "established unblamable in holiness before God," so as to resemble in a moral and exalted sense those immortal beings in heaven who are here called the "glorious body" of Christ. The body to be changed embraces both Jew and Gentile christians, who were at that time to be raised from their lowly condition into his gospel kingdom and "shine forth like the sun." This is evident from the manner in which he commences: "For our conversation is in *heaven*, from *whence* we look for the Saviour, the Lord Jesus Christ, who shall change our *lowly body* that it maybe fashioned like unto his glorious body." He contrasts the low and oppressed condition of the whole christian body with what will be their exalted condition at the coming of Christ, and that exalted condition will assemble that glorified body of beings in *heaven* who died in his cause, and with whom they had their conversation, and from *whence* they were expecting the Saviour. It has reference, I conceive, to the body in which Christ arose. The church is the body of Christ, and it is to be presented to himself a *glorious body*, not having spot, wrinkle, or any such thing. The Greek word *tapeinos* rendered "vile," should be rendered *lowly or humble.*

It will be noticed, by the reader, that the word *body* is used in the *singular* number and not in the plural, as some have quoted it in their writings. But if it refer to individual *forms*, it ought to be rendered in the *plural*—"who shall change our vile *bodies."* But it means the whole church or body of believers—a collective body of individuals. In this sense the Greek word, *soma*, here rendered *body* is frequently used in the New Testament. That the apostle does not refer to all mankind is evident from the fact, that after the vile body is changed according to the working, he adds—whereby he is able *even* to subdue all things unto himself—That is, able *even* to subdue all things as well as to change that body. If the passage refer to an immortal and general resurrection, or rather to the change of all the living into immortal beings, then there would be none to subdue after that period. But if we apply it to the coming of Christ in that generation, and to the change of the whole christian body, then all is plain and in perfect agreement with the preceding and succeeding context; also with 1 Cor. 15th chapter, and with the whole tenor of revelation, which speaks of but *one coming* of our Saviour in his kingdom, and which shows that the work of subjection commenced after the change of the living at the last trump, whose sound announced the commencement of his reign. The word *kai*, rendered *even*, should probably have been rendered *also*. "Who shall change our lowly body—according to the working whereby he is able also to subdue all things to himself." The whole context, however, justifies the above exposition because the christians were looking for the coming of Christ at the end of that age, and exclaimed, "the Lord is at hand."

[To be continued.]

SERMON XXIII

"For as in Adam all die, even so in Christ shall all be made alive." 1 Cor. xv:20.

In our last we noticed the context, and also taken into consideration the language of Paul on the coming of Christ and the change of the living in Phil. iii:20, 21. This, we have shown, has no reference to the mortal bodies of men being changed to immortal bodies, so as to resemble the personal form of Jesus Christ. If it refer to Jesus, still the resemblance would be *moral, not personal*, for no where do the scriptures teach, that we are in our personal appearance to be like our Saviour. But in a *moral* sense, "we shall be like him, for we shall see him as he is." I do not say, that there will be no *personal* resemblance between immortal beings and Christ. I fully believe there will be; but I mean that this personal resemblance is more a matter of course, than a doctrine of divine revelation. I do not read of the "glorious body" of Jesus in his immortal resurrection state. But the scriptures do compare the moral body of Christians on earth with the glorified body of holy beings in heaven, Heb. xii:22, 23—"But ye are come unto mount Zion, and unto the city of the living God, the heavenly Jerusalem, and to an in-numerable company of angels to the general assembly and church of the first-born, which are written in heaven, and to God the judge of all, and to the spirits of just men made made perfect." So far as the Christians were "established unblamable in holiness before God even our Father at the coming of our Lord Jesus Christ with all his saints" so far as they were elevated to "shine as the brightness of the firmament and as the stars forever" so far as their moral condition and enjoyments were improved and enlarged, thus far, of course, the *lowly body* of the church on earth would be changed into a moral resemblance of that "glorious body" of Christ, who were praising him in heaven. In *heaven* the Christians had their conversation, from whence they were looking for the Saviour, as shortly to come, and fashion them into a moral resemblance of those saints above, who had died in his cause, and who were to come with him. From the whole context, the conclusion is irresistible that this change of the "vile body" was at the coming of the Lord *then* at hand, and not at the end of time, as some imagine.

Another scripture commonly applied to the *general* resurrection of the dead, and a change of all the living is recorded in 1 Thess. iv:15, 16, 17—"For this we say unto you by the word of the Lord, that we which are alive and remain unto the coming of the Lord shall not *be before* them that are asleep. For the Lord himself shall descend from heaven with a shout, with the voice of the archangel and the trump of God; and the *dead in Christ* shall rise first. Then we which are alive and remain shall be caught up together with them in the clouds to meet the Lord in air, and so we shall be evermore with the Lord."

That Paul here refers to the coming of Christ in his kingdom to establish his reign, and to elevate the Christians who were alive at that period, the *preceding* and *succeeding* contexts fully justify. And so I must understand his language, till some one can prove a third coming of Christ, and an *eighth* sounding trump at the end of time. In the two preceding chapters, he dwells largely upon the persecutions of the Christians, exhorts them to be faithful, expresses his desire "to perfect that which is lacking in their faith," and concludes by saying—"To the end he may establish your hearts unblamable in holiness before God, even our Father, at the coming of our Lord Jesus Christ *with all his saints."* No one will deny that this has reference to his coming at the end of the Jewish age. Now would it not be doing injustice to this powerful and cogent reasoner to say, that he suddenly drops this subject without giving his brethren any warning, and runs off to the end of time, speaks of another coming of Christ at which he is to raise, at the same instant, all the dead and change the living to immortal beings? And that he should again, as suddenly, drop this subject, and hasten right back to the coming of Christ at the destruction of Jerusalem? To charge him with this is certainly ungenerous.

After stating that Christ should descend with a shout, with the voice of the archangel and the trump of God to exalt the dead and living, he adds—"But of the times and seasons, brethren, ye have no need that I write for yourselves perfectly know that the day of the Lord so cometh as a thief in the night. For when they shall say peace and safety then sudden destruction cometh upon them, and they shall not escape." There is no resisting the conclusion, that *"the day of the Lord"* in this passage refers to the same period when *"the Lord himself shall descend from heaven"* in the passage above; which must be at the destruction of Jerusalem. He quotes Christ's own language, Matt. xxiv:43. See also 2 Peter iii:10. In both places, the sudden coming of Jesus is compared to a "thief in the night." But where is a *general* resurrection, at the end of time, clearly stated, that he had no need to inform them of the times and seasons, because they already perfectly knew? Where is sudden destruction to come upon any in that day? For one, I find no such revelation.

Though the doctrine of immortal resurrection of all mankind was fully revealed, and established in the world at the coming of Christ in his kingdom; yet that particular point is not argued by the apostle in the scripture on which we are commenting. He is not speaking of all mankind, nor of the immortal resurrection; but as in Phil. iii:20, 21, so *here* he is speaking of the Christians *only* who should be alive when that scene burst and of those dead *only* who had died in the cause of Christ. "The dead in Christ" cannot possibly include those who died previous to his birth, but those only who died in the faith of his doctrine previous to his coming in his kingdom. We might reason this point at large, but deem it unnecessary till some one proves how those, who never heard of a Saviour, could be said to die in Christ, or to be dead in him. I would, however, remark that the Greek preposition *en* may be rendered, *on account of*. The phrase would then read thus—*the dead on account of Christ*. Wakefield renders it thus—"*they who have died in the cause of Christ*." That this is its true sense, I have not a doubt.

Let one thing here be distinctly noticed: Paul says—"For this we say unto you by the word of the Lord, that we which are alive and remain," &c. Now where has our Lord ever said, when speaking of the immortal resurrection, that some would be alive, and be changed to immortal beings? Nowhere. This single circumstance ought to make every man pause before he asserts such a change to be true. Read Christ's language in all three of the Evangelists where he addresses the Sadducees; and he speaks only of the dead being raised, but not of any one being changed. Read his language, John vi:39—"And this is the Father's will which hath sent me, that of all which he hath given me I should lose nothing, but raise it up again at the last day." Nothing is here said about changing the living to immortal beings. The Father has given all into the hands of his Son; and if he is to *raise* them up at the last day, then all must die, for the *change* of the living is not the *resurrection* of the dead. How then could Paul tell his brethren, "by the word of the Lord," that they were to be thus changed? He could not because there is not a "thus saith the Lord" to support it. But Paul had the word of the Lord support the change in the living which we have pointed out. Christ said, "the righteous should go into life eternal," they "that endured unto the end should be saved" that "they should shine like the sun in the kingdom of their Father," and that "they should be recompensed at the resurrection of the just."

But, inquires the reader, were those who died in the cause of Christ raised immortal at his coming? No, they were not. It simply means that they were in that day to receive their elevated stations of glory and and honor in the gospel kingdom, so much so, as if they had been alive. The living Christians, in this respect, were not to be before them. Having suffered and died in the cause of Christ, they were in the minds of the living to "shine as the stars forever and ever" in the kingdom of Christ, because they had turned many to righteousness. The Lord had, as it were, delayed his coming, and many had given up faith in Christ's resurrection, and were sorrowing without hope over their friends who had fallen asleep in his cause. They of course had no faith in the immortal resurrection of their friends, nor in the fulfillment of Christ's predicted coming to raise their names to unfading honor for having labored and died in his cause. We are not to understand that those departed saints were *literally* exalted to elevated stations in Christ's kingdom on earth, any more than Christ *literally* came. But as Jesus was *in that day*, at the end of the Jewish age, "crowned with glory and honor," as king on the mediatorial throne of the universe, so were his apostles elevated on thrones of glory with him. Jesus says, "when the Son of man shall sit on his throne of glory, ye also shall also sit upon twelve thrones, judging the twelve tribes of Israel."

Now certain it is, that Jesus did take his throne, when he came in his glory, at the destruction of the temple. Then it is equally certain, that the apostles and martyrs also took their's at the same period and in the same sense. *Then* Christ came and "his holy angels" and all the saints came with him; not literally, but in the same sense that he himself came. Luke ix:26, 27—"For whosoever shall be ashamed of me and of my words, of him shall the Son of Man be ashamed when he shall come in his own glory and of his Father's and of the holy angels; but I tell you of a truth there be some standing here which shall not taste death till they see the kingdom of God." I Thess. iii:13—"To the end he may establish your hearts unblamable in holiness before God our Lord even our Father, at the coming of our Lord Jesus Christ with all his saints." Here we perceive, that he was to come "*with all his saints and holy angels*." By his *holy angels*, we are to understand his gospel messengers or martyred apostles and by *his* saints, those who had died in his cause. These are the persons who are said to be *dead in Christ, and asleep in Jesus*. By the words *dead and asleep* we are not to understand their present extinction of existence in contrast with their immortal resurrection, but the supposed *low and disgraceful* cause in which they died, or for which they were put to death by their persecutors, as malefactors. This *disgraceful condition*, in which their murderers viewed them as unchangeably sleeping, stands in contrast with their *triumphant exaltation* at the coming of Christ. Their enemies would *then* look upon them as having come forth from the dust of the earth and shining as the brightness of the firmament and as the stars forever and ever, and not as sleeping in perpetual infamy and dishonor. [See Daniel xii 2, 3, and John v:28, 29.] Their enemies (whether dead or alive) were to come forth to *shame, contempt, and condemnation*, which stand in contrast with the *glory and honor* to which the Christians (whether dead or alive in Christ) were to be raised in the minds of the living even to succeeding generations.

Let it be distinctly noticed that *these dead in Christ* are not said to be raised *incorruptible and immortal*, but only caught up with the living Christians in the clouds to meet the Lord in the air—not *literally*, but in the same sense that the living saw the Son of man coming in the clouds of heaven, so should they see his saints and holy angels raised from the slumber of infamy, and, together with the Christians who remained alive at that day, be exalted with him in the air. [See Matt. xxiv:30, 31—Mark xiii:26, 27—Luke xxi:27, 28, and Rev. i:7.] In these passages he is represented as "coming in the *clouds* with his angels," who "gathered, with a great sound of the trumpet, his elect," and raised them to honor in his kingdom. And let me add—this is all the *change* Christ has ever said should take place in the living at the sound of the Trumpet. I have no doubt that the Apostle had his eye upon the above words of our Lord when he said, "we shall be caught up in the clouds to meet the Lord in the air." It will here be plainly seen in what sense those who had died in the cause of Christ were *first* raised. They are represented as coming with him at the destruction of the temple, and after that event the whole "body" was exalted together. The "vile body" of Christians on earth (vile indeed in the eyes of their enemies) was then "fashioned like unto his glorious body" of saints and angels in heaven who had died in his cause.

That we have given a correct exposition of 1 Thess. iv:15, 16, 17, is evident from Paul's words 2 Tim. iv:7, 8—"I have fought the good fight, I have finished my course, I have kept the faith. Henceforth there is laid up for me a *crown of righteousness*, which the Lord, the righteous Judge shall give me at *that day*," &c. The phrase "*that day*" means not the day of Paul's death, but the day Christ should appear in the clouds of heaven at the end of the Jewish age. His *crown was merited* for having "fought the good fight and kept the faith." The crown means that exalted honor he should then receive for having "turned many to righteousness." And not only himself, but all, "who love the appearing of Christ," should shine as the brightness of the firmament and as the stars forever and ever in his gospel kingdom among men. We this day look upon the martyrs and apostles as the lights of the Christian world and as occupying, on the sacred page, stations far more exalted than any ever conferred upon the greatest men of the universe. They are "made priests and kings to God" for dying in his cause, and thus establishing the truth of Christianity.

This was the "first resurrection," and these were the persons who had a part in it, which no subsequent christians can ever can have. Rev. xx:6—"Blessed and holy is he that hath part in the first resurrection, on such the second death hath no power, but they shall be priests of God and of Christ, and shall reign with him a thousand years." But if Christ had not come in his kingdom at the end of the Jewish age, as the prophets and himself had declared, then the whole Christian system must have fallen and the names of its martyrs and apostles remained buried in perpetual infamy as a set of deluded men and impostors. But, blessed be God, it is not so. They, by their faithfulness, have attained unto the "first resurrection" and thus broken the dark chains of infidelity into fragments. This is the *resurrection and change* referred to in Phil. iii:20, 21, and 1 Thess. iv:15, 16, 17, on which we have commented.

We have intentionally omitted till now Phil. iii:11, 12, as our ideas will be more readily comprehended here than in our introductory discourse, where we simply adverted to these words of Paul—"If by any means I might attain unto the resurrection of the dead—Not as though I had already attained either were already perfect," &c. Here we perceive that the resurrection unto which he desired to attain depended on his exertions in the cause of Christ, and being faithful unto the end. He says (verse 14)—"I press towards the mark for the prize of the high calling of God in Christ Jesus." But what prize was this? Ans. It was a *part* in the *first resurrection* to which he desired to attain (verse 11) and he was not "perfect," he feared "lest after having preached to others himself might be a cast-away." He feared that he might not endure faithful unto the end. He was well aware that the promise was—"Be thou faithful unto death and I will give thee a crown of life." To obtain this crown of life in the first resurrection, was the *highest prize*, the *highest calling of God*, ever suspended upon human merits! Paul did continue faithful, and as he was led to the thought of death, with composure and satisfaction exclaimed— "For I am now ready to be offered; and the time of my departure" is at hand. "I have fought the good fight, I have finished my course, I have kept the faith; henceforth there is laid up for me a *crown of righteousness*, which the Lord the righteous Judge shall give me at that day, and not to me only, but unto all them also, that love his appearing." Here we perceive that Paul had continued faithful, and was entitled to the promised crown, which was awarded to him, and to all "the dead in Christ," who, on account of their faithfulness, had a part in the first resurrection—when he came in the clouds of heaven to establish his kingdom. It has nothing to do with the immortal resurrection of the dead, for that is not the reward of merit, but the gift of God. To *that* all shall attain who die in Adam. But in the *first* resurrection none had a part except those who died in the cause of Christ, and the living who continued faithful to the day of his appearing. On them and *them only* devolved the honor of establishing the truth of Christianity for the happiness of future generations, by not only testifying that they had seen Jesus alive from the dead, but by cheerfully submitting to death, and showing themselves miracles of suffering in his cause. Both the departed and those that remained alive, attained to the first resurrection, were glorified together, and their crowns shall shine in the gospel heavens with undiminished splendor long after those of kings and tyrants shall be dimmed and lost in the vortex of revolutions.

He concludes the chapter by noticing the change of the "vile body" which we have explained. Here then is no evidence of a general resurrection, nor of the end of time. The *context*, the *silence* of Jesus about the change of the living into immortal beings, and the *whole tenor* of revelation combine to set it at defiance. Of one thing I am satisfied; that no man ever *has*, and I believe, no man ever *can reconcile* the change of the living and the resurrection of the dead recorded in Philippians and 1 Thessalonians with their respective contexts, so as to prove a general and immortal resurrection at the end of time. As I have traveled in an untrodden path, I do not know but that I may have erred in some minor points, but am satisfied that my general positions are sound and tenable.

[To be continued.]

SERMON XXIV

"For as in Adam all die, even so in Christ shall all be made alive." 1 Cor. xv:20.

We have now come to that point in our subject where it will be necessary to cite a few passages to prove that the immortal resurrection is *successive, not general,* and will conclude by considering some of the principal texts, which may be urged as objections.

We have already shown that the resurrection of the dead was to be at the sound of the last trump. And as that trump commenced sounding at the end of the Jewish age, when Christ came in his kingdom, I deem it sufficient to establish the fact that the dead are continually rising in this *last, this gospel day.* But the question presents itself— were any of the human family raised immortal before that period? To this question I give an affirmative answer. I firmly believe, that the dead have been rising immortal from Adam to the present day, for God has never changed the established order of the universe. I believe that the dead are raised without any *miracle,* in the common acceptance of that term, as much as I believe that we are born, and die, not by a *miracle,* but according to that constitution of things which God has immutably established from the beginning. I believe this doctrine of Christ to be founded upon the unchanging principles of philosophy but so mysterious, that man in his present existence cannot comprehend the subtle causes and effects by which he shall put on immortality. It was, therefore, necessary that this sublime truth should be established in the world by the miracles Jesus wrought and by the miraculous power of God in raising him from death. The first man Adam was made by a miracle, while his posterity are naturally born into life, according to that constitution of things which God has established. So Christ, the second Adam, was born from the dead by a miracle, while mankind from the beginning, have, in succession, been born from the dead according to that constitution of things which he has established.

On this principle, it may be stated as an objection, that as none of Adam's posterity could be born till their parent was created by a miracle, so none of the human family could be born from the dead, till Christ the second Adam were raised immortal by the miraculous power of God. This objection is futile unless it can be proved that Christ *creates* life and immortality. In fact, it would even then fail;— because Christ, as our sacrifice, was slain from the foundation of the world in the offerings made to God in his stead. The atonement, made by the high priest throughout the whole Mosaic dispensation, concluded by raising the Jewish nation in figure on his "breastplate of judgment" into the holy of holies, which was a pattern of things in the heavens. The atonement always involved the resurrection. The judgment of the Jews, for two thousand years, by Moses only pointed out the resurrection of man in *figure*, but Christ proved the *reality* by a tangible *fact*, and thus revealed it to the living as the doctrine of God of which the world had been ignorant. So what the *judgment* of the world by Moses taught in *figure*, *the judgment* of the world by Christ teaches in *reality*. My limits will not allow me to argue this point at large. I have already remarked, that I believe *"the judgment of the world"* expresses the whole reign of Christ including the resurrection.

We now proceed to notice the Scriptures. Matt. xxii. 31, 32.

"But as touching the resurrection of the dead, have ye not read that which was spoken unto you by God, saying, I am the God of Abraham, the God of Isaac and the God of Jacob? God is not the God of the dead, but of the living."

To this Luke adds, "*for all live unto him.*" In order to make these words of Jesus refer to a general resurrection at the end of time, all writers have availed themselves of this last clause in Luke (on which Matthew and Mark are silent) and contend that it means—all live unto God who in his counsels views the future resurrection as present. But this exposition by no means satisfies my mind. If Abraham, Issac and Jacob are not raised—if they are yet wrapped in the insensibility of death, then God during that period is not their God.

To illustrate this, we would remark, that Jehovah could not be Creator till something were created by him. He could not be Father till he had an offspring. He could not be Lord till he possessed property;— neither could he be God till there were a worshipper. *Jehovah* is the only abstract name he could possess, were he solitary and without a universe. All the other names ascribed to him are relative. The name God as much pre-supposes the actual existence of a *worshipper* as that of father does the actual existence of a *child*. Remove the *child*, and the once doating parent is no longer to him a father. God is not, therefore, the God of the dead, for as such, they could not worship him. He is, however, Lord of both the dead and the living claiming them as his property. Abraham, Issac and Jacob were therefore alive, and worshipping him when those words were spoken to Moses, for in no other sense could he have been their God any more than he was before they were born. The phrase "*for all live unto him,*" may, in this instance, embrace only the three patriarchs, as no others are involved in the quotation. The Sadducees believed in the writings of Moses only, and it is not at all probable, that Jesus referred to any persons, not mentioned by Moses, as it would have been no proof to the Sadducees. His argument is, to prove that the three patriarchs, *are raised* according to their own writings, not *shall be raised*. Now that the *dead are raised* Moses showed at the bush when he called God the God of Abraham, Isaac and Jacob. Here we perceive that "*the dead*" refers to the three persons whom Moses showed were raised. He then adds—for he is not the God of the *dead* but of the *living*, for all live unto him—that is, the three patriarchs *all* live to him. If the phrase embrace any others, it must be the living in eternity, not the living in the flesh nor the dead as such. It would make Jesus contradict himself in the same breath. "He is not the God of the *dead*, but of the *living*, for *all* live unto him." To whom does this "*all*" refer? To the "*living*"; not the "*dead*," for in that case he would be the God of the dead.

Luke ix. 30. "*And behold there talked with him two men, which were Moses and Elias.*" The transfiguration of our Lord is recorded also by both Matthew and Mark, and it is plainly stated that the disciples "saw his glory and the two men that stood with him." If Moses and Elias were dead, their bodies crumbled to dust, and their minds in a state of insensibility, then they were not Moses and Elias who talked with him. Even if God had represented those two persons by other forms, they could no more have been Moses and Elias than Adam and Noah. It is *consciousness and memory* which constitute personal identity; and if a conversation was carried on with Jesus by any means that human ingenuity can invent, while Moses and Elias were wrapped in as profound insensibility as the dust with which their bodies mingled, then it could not have been Moses and Elias who conversed with Jesus any more than if they had never had an existence. Perhaps it may be said that, as it is called a *vision* by Matthew, it might have been nothing *real*. But as the word *horama* means a *sight* as well as *vision*, and as the other Evangelists do represent it as an actual appearance and nothing visionary, it is to be taken in this sense. Was it not a *reality* that the three disciples saw Jesus transfigured, and though in that condition was it not still their *identical* Lord? Certainly. Then the vision was so far *real*, and I see no ground on which the other personages can be considered phantoms. Mark says, "he charged them that they should tell no man *what things they had seen*," &c. See also Luke ix. 36. Here it is made certain that it was not an appearance in a dream, but a real and visible sight of three persons whose names are given. Consequently Moses and Elias were there as certain as was Jesus Christ. If so, they must have been raised from the dead, for man can have no conscious existence hereafter in a disembodied state. The scriptures teach that the resurrection is our only hope of a future conscious state of being. As to the translation of Elijah we shall not here notice it.

Phil. i. 23, 24. "*For I am in a strait betwixt two, having a desire to depart and be with Christ which is far better; nevertheless to abide in the flesh is more needful for you.*" To depart and be with Christ must, I conceive, mean in the resurrection world, for in no other sense could he be with Christ so as to render his condition "far better." Nothing can be *good or bad* for a man in a state of perfect insensibility, any more than for a man unborn—Neither could he be with Christ in such a State, any more than before he existed. Between the condition of a man in non-existence [pardon the expression] and in life, no comparison as to enjoyment or suffering can possibly be drawn. The apostle therefore draws a comparison between his present condition of conscious existence with his brethren, and his future condition of conscious existence with Christ which was far better.

That Paul has reference, in the above, to an immortal existence in the resurrection, is evident from 2 Cor. v. 1, 2, 3, 4.

"For we know that if our earthly house of this tabernacle were dissolved, we have a building of God, a house not made with hands eternal in the heavens. For in this we groan, earnestly desiring to be clothed upon with our house which is from heaven. If so be that being clothed we shall not be found naked. For we that are in this tabernacle do groan, being burdened, not for that we would be unclothed, but clothed upon, that mortality might be swallowed up of life."

If the above do not prove that the apostle expected to be clothed upon with his house from heaven shortly after his earthly tabernacle were dissolved, then I must acknowledge my ignorance of his meaning. He desires not to be unclothed so as to be found naked at the coming of Christ. By this I understand that between death and the resurrection there is a state of insensibility of several days duration, while the spiritual body is putting on, and if he died so near the coming of Christ, that the process was not completed, and mortality not swallowed up of life, he would be found naked, i.e. In the state of the dead. He therefore expresses no desire to be found unclothed at that period but clothed upon and present with Christ. This is evident from verses 6, and 7.

"Therefore we are always confident, knowing that whilst we are at home in the body we are absent from the Lord. We are confident, I say, and willing rather to be absent from the body and present with the Lord."

While in the body, though they had many consolations in the faith of Christ, though "he was with them always even unto the end of the age," though "to live was Christ," yet this condition he terms being *absent* from the Lord in comparison to being *present* with him, which cannot mean in the unclothed state of insensibility, but where "mortality is swallowed up of life."

Let it be distinctly noticed, that the apostle is speaking of three states—

1st. as being in this earthly house or body where they were absent from the Lord—

2nd. as being unclothed and found naked at his coming for which they had no desire—

3rd. As being absent from the body and present with the Lord where they should be clothed upon with their house from heaven that mortality might be swallowed up of life, for which they had a desire.

Verse 9. "*Wherefore we labor that whether present or absent we may be accepted of him.*" Here we perceive that they did not labor to obtain entrance into his presence, because the immortal resurrection is the gift of God. But they labored, whether *alive* on earth or *immortal* in heaven, that they might be accepted among those, who were worthy to obtain a crown of righteousness in the first resurrection for having continued faithful unto the end—that they might be worthy to form a part of that glorious body of witnesses in heaven who were slain for the testimony of Jesus. And the body of christians on earth, who continued faithful to the coming of Christ, were to be fashioned like those above, and receive the same exalted honor in his gospel kingdom, and the whole compose one bright body of infallible witnesses, whose testimony can never be shaken by all the powers infidelity. "To depart and be with Christ which is far better" must mean in an immortal existence.

We cannot, for want of room, argue this part of our subject at large; —but the above is in perfect agreement with the philosophy of St. Paul, (1 Cor. 15,) where he compares the raising of the spiritual body to a grain of wheat sown in the earth. I would not be understood to say that this natural body of flesh and blood is ever to rise. No one, I presume, will contend that infants, youth and decrepid age, and those who are born deformed will be raised in that condition and all retain their various complexions. I believe, however, that there are those subtle materials in the natural body which, when extricated from the earthly tenement, and completely developed, shall produce the immortal being; and that these are as perfect in the infant as in the man.

We will now conclude by anticipating and answering one or two principal objections. It may be objected that, if any one arose immortal before Christ, he could not have been "the first-born from the dead" as stated in Col. i. 18. This does not mean *first* in the order of time, but in *rank*. It means *principal*, and is explained by the connecting phrase—"that in all things he might have the *pre-eminence*." It is more particularly explained in Rev. i. 5. "Jesus Christ the faithful witness and the first-begotten of the dead and the Prince of the kings of the earth." In connexion with this, we will introduce 1 Cor. xv. 20. "But now is Christ risen from the dead and become *first-fruits* of them that slept." This also has reference to *rank* and not to *first* in the order of time. In evidence of this, we will quote Cruden,—"The day after the feast of the

Passover, they brought a sheaf into the temple the *first-fruits* of the barley-harvest. The sheaf was threshed in the court, and of the grain that came out they took a full homer; i.e. About three pints. After it had been well winnowed, parched and bruised, they sprinkled over it a log of oil; i.e. Near a pint. They added to it a handful of incense; and the priest that received this offering shook it before the Lord towards the four quarters of the world; he cast part of it upon the altar and the rest was his own. After this every one might begin their harvest. This was offered in the name of the whole nation, and by *this* the harvest was sanctified unto them."

Here let the question be asked—Was this sheaf called the *first-fruits* because it was ripe before the whole harvest? No; it was not cut till the harvest was ripe. Was it called *first* because the harvest would be *second* in following it to the temple to be presented to God, by the priest, in the presence of the people? No; it was not to be carried to the temple, nor would the priest or the people ever see the whole harvest thus dedicated to God. But it was called "the *first* of the ripe fruits," because it was offered to God in the presence of the people as an evidence of the consecration of the whole harvest throughout the nation. It was *first* in distinction, or *importance* without any allusion whatever to *first* in the order of time.

So "Christ was the *chosen* of God, the *elect precious*, and the *Son* consecrated forevermore." He was "the chief among ten thousand" and proved to be the Son of God with power by a resurrection from the dead without seeing corruption. In this condition he was presented to the people as an evidence of the resurrection and consecration of all mankind. In this he was *first and last*—that is, the *principal*, the *chief, the head*, and in *this* he never *has had*, and never *will have a second* in the order of time. This is no evidence therefore that he was the first one who ever rose to an immortal existence. We have positive proof that Moses and Elias were raised from the dead, an in a state of conscious existence for they conversed with our Lord in the presence of three of his disciples. They appeared in glory, and were two as real personages on the one part, as was our Saviour on the other.

Acts xxvi. 23. *"That Christ should suffer, and that he should be the first that should rise from the dead, and should shew light to the people and to the Gentiles."* This passage contains, perhaps, as plausible an objection against my views as any that can be produced. But this passage means, that Christ should be the *first* who should show light to the Jews and Gentiles through a resurrection from the dead. The Greek word, here rendered "*should rise*," is anastaseos from *anastasis*. It is a *substantive*, not a *verb*. Professor Leusden, in his Latin Testament, renders it "*ex resurrectione mortuorum*"—*by a resurrection from the dead.* The verb, *to raise, is egeiro*, and is six times applied to the raising of Christ from the dead in 1 Cor xv. *Anistemi* also means *to rise* and is applied to raising the dead to life. But neither—anistemi nor egeiro_ are used in the verse, but *anastaseos*—

Consequently it cannot *literally* be rendered "*should rise,*" but *resurrection*. Wakefield translates it thus—"That Christ would suffer death and would be the *first* to proclaim salvation to this people and the Gentiles *by a resurrection from the dead.*" This is evidently the real sense of the passage, and I shall offer upon it no further comment.
